HISTAMINE INTOLERANCE
COOKBOOK

Delicious, Nourishing, Low-Histamine Recipes, And Every Ingredient Labeled For Histamine Content

TONY WRIGHTON

Copyright © 2024 Tony Wrighton

All rights reserved. No part of this guide may be reproduced in any form without permission in writing from the publisher except in the case of brief quotations embodied in critical articles or reviews.

Legal & Disclaimer

The information contained in this book is not designed to replace or take the place of any form of medicine or professional medical advice. The information in this book has been provided for educational and entertainment purposes only.

The information contained in this book has been compiled from sources deemed reliable, and it is accurate to the best of the Author's knowledge; however, the Author cannot guarantee its accuracy and validity and cannot be held liable for any errors or omissions. Changes are periodically made to this book. You must consult your doctor or get professional medical advice before using any of the suggested remedies, techniques, or information in this book.

Upon using the information contained in this book, you agree to hold harmless the Author, and Publisher, from and against any damages, costs, and expenses, including any legal fees potentially resulting from the application of any of the information provided by this guide. This disclaimer applies to any damages or injury caused by the use and application, whether directly or indirectly, of any advice or information presented, whether for breach of contract, tort, negligence, personal injury, criminal intent, or under any other cause of action.

You agree to accept all risks of using the information presented inside this book. You need to consult a professional medical practitioner in order to ensure you are both able and healthy enough to participate in this program.

Contents

INTRODUCTION 9
    The Story So Far 9
    What to Expect 10
    It's Partly About Self-Interest! 12
    A Unique Approach to Low Histamine Recipes 12
    References and Principle Sources for Histamine Diet Information 12
    One of the Great Pleasures of Life 14

WHAT IS HISTAMINE INTOLERANCE? 17

WHY FOLLOW A LOW-HISTAMINE DIET? 18
    Foods High in Histamine 18

THE LOW-HISTAMINE FOOD LIST 20
    DISCLAIMER: Always check with your doctor or health practitioner before starting any new diet. This list is not advice; it is intended for information and discussion only.
    Low-Histamine Foods 20
    Medium-Histamine Foods 23
    High-Histamine Foods 26
    A Quick Note on Coffee 28

BREAKFAST RECIPES 30
    Apple and Pumpkin Seed Granola 31
    Carrot Cake Porridge 33
    Maple Coconut Granola 35
    Breakfast Blackberry and Chia Pudding 37
    Butter Coffee with Rosemary 39
    Maple Cherry Chia Pudding 41
    Blueberry Quinoa Bake 42
    Vegetarian Granola Breakfast Pizza 44

Breakfast Granola with Coconut Cream 46
Sweet Potato and Corn Hash 48
Cauliflower Bread 50
Blackberry, Oat and Coconut Smoothie 52
Blueberry Breakfast Smoothie 53
Melon, Peach and Chia Smoothie 55
Green Breakfast Power Smoothie 57
Apple Pie Smoothie 58
Sweet Melon Smoothie 59
"Hidden Health" Smoothie 61
Cherry Smoothie 62

SNACKS RECIPES 64
Burger Bites 65
Oven-Baked Apple Trail Mix 67
Homemade Sweet Potato Chips 68
Maca Coconut Cream with Blueberries 70
Herbed Oat Crackers 72
Pumpkin Seed Butter 74

SOUP RECIPES 76
Butternut Squash and Turmeric Soup 77
Wild Rice Vegetable Soup 79
Sweet Potato Quinoa Soup 81
Classic Pumpkin Soup 83
Sumptuous Celery Soup 84
Carrot and Sage Soup 86
Cabbage and Zucchini Soup 88
Creamy Broccoli Soup 90
Soffritto Broccoli Soup 92

MAIN DISH RECIPES 93
Instant Pot Beef Shin 94
Tasty Chicken Wings 96
"Yum Chicken" with Cottage Cheese and
Rosemary 97

Contents

Oven Baked Chicken and Zucchini Toast with Herbs and Cheese 99
Organic Beef with Herb-Based Topping 101
Honey, Rosemary, and Butter Roast Chicken with Pea Shoot Salad 103
Oven-Baked Whole Chicken with Mint, Basil, Zucchini and Black Rice 105
Seared and Baked Lamb with Vegetables 107
Sweet Paprika Crusted Cod 109
Vegan Power Dinner 111
Maple Baked Ricotta and Butternut Squash 113
Zucchini, Basil, and Mint Rice Pasta 115
Butternut Squash Gnocchi 117
Coconut Quinoa Risotto 119
Cheesy Baked Butternut Squash Risotto 120
Honey Roasted Pumpkin Quinoa 122
Cherry, Blackberry, Cottage Cheese Salad 124
Rice, Pea Shoot and Pomegranate Salad 126

SECRET SAUCES 128
Low-Histamine Ketchup 129
No-Yogurt Honey Mint Dip 131
Pomegranate, Garlic and Ginger Salad Sauce 132
Sweet Paprika Spiced Tahini Dressing 133

DRINKS RECIPES 134
Fiery Carrot and Turmeric Juice 135
Celery and Ginger Juice 136
Ginger and Green Apple Drink 137
Sweet Melon and Cucumber Smoothie 138
Basil and Blackberry Potion 139
Sweet Melon, Peach, and Chia Smoothie 141

DESSERT RECIPES 142
Uncle Steve's Caribbean Pone 143
Histahappy Slice 146

Blackberry and Cherry Crisp 148
Blueberry "Ice Cream" 150
Blackberry Coconut Popsicles 151
Chia Jam 153

LIST OF INGREDIENTS USED 154

FINAL WORDS 157

WHAT'S NEXT? 160

INTRODUCTION

- Are avocados allowed on the Histamine Diet?
- Is chocolate high-histamine or low-histamine?
- Can I have a glass of red wine with my dinner?
- How can I live without tomato ketchup?

The Low-Histamine Diet is an absolute minefield and these are all questions I get asked regularly. And so I am delighted you've bought this Histamine Intolerance Cookbook. After the success of Histamine Intolerance Explained, I realized there was a need for a guide where good, low-histamine diet information and recipes all came together. So, here it is.

The Story So Far

This cookbook was originally published under my company name, Ketoko Guides, all the way back in 2020. This was a name I adopted for my specialized series of health books. The idea was to allow me to work with a small team and specifically address an audience interested in health and nutrition. This approach differed a bit from my previous, "normal" books (!), where I've been fortunate to have some success.

There was only one problem with Ketoko Guides. Everyone knew it was me behind the books. The histamine intolerance world is small, and after all I made no secret of the fact that I'd published it with my talented team. So who was I trying to kid?

And there was another thing. Since 2020, I've connected with a surprising number of individuals dealing with histamine intolerance through instagram and my website. You wouldn't believe how high the number of daily inquiries is, often coming from people who've found any mention of histamine intolerance to their practitioner is met with blank looks—or worse—outright derision. I personally respond to these people and often recommend this book's special feature where every ingredient is labeled for histamine intolerance. It is a valuable starting point for many and was another reason for me to put my name to a refined and refreshed edition of The Histamine Intolerance Cookbook.

I'd still like to pay massive tribute to all the writers, fact-checkers, editors, recipe-testers and experts who helped in the making of this book. In particular, Claire G (@lowhistaminekitchen on Instagram) who helped create and refine some of the recipes. It's working with people like Claire that is so important, as I want this cookbook to be the absolute best resource for histamine intolerance, and tried and tested by the best chefs and cooks out there. She is fantastic. Please do follow her content.

Finally, I very much hope that we can eventually bring out a third edition, in full colour, with pictures of all the recipes. I know that many of you would love that, but it would take time and money, so it's something to save up for, or consider involving a big publisher.

What to Expect

In this Histamine Intolerance Cookbook, I start by going over – briefly – Histamine Intolerance and why it might affect you. But I know that you already might have looked

Introduction

into all that, duh – you bought a Histamine Intolerance Cookbook. So without further ado, I move straight on to the world's most respected dietary information regarding histamine content in food. You can come back to the Histamine Food List again and again – I find it particularly useful when out in restaurants, perusing menus, and planning a new dish.

And then on to the recipes. I've packed this cookbook with delicious, nourishing recipes, and every ingredient is labeled for histamine content. Mouthwatering recipes like...

- OVEN BAKED CHICKEN AND ZUCCHINI TOAST with herbs and histamine-friendly cheese
- MAPLE-BAKED RICOTTA AND BUTTERNUT SQUASH - a taste explosion
- BLUEBERRY QUINOA BAKE topped with creamy coconut and golden flaxseed
- HOMEMADE LOW-HISTAMINE KETCHUP - better than the real thing!
- JUICES, SMOOTHIES AND POTIONS formulated especially to lower your histamine bucket

With sections on breakfasts, starters, main courses, low-histamine meat dishes, desserts, and secret sauces, as well as histamine-lowering snacks (often tricky for us histamine people, but not now), you'll learn to celebrate and love food again on the low histamine diet. You'll also find special extra nuggets dotted throughout the book, where I talk in a bit more detail about some of my favourite ingredients such as pea shoots, flaxseed and celery. Some of these magical foods can help to lower your histamine levels all on their own, and nourish you at the same time. I also look at kitchen tech that can help with histamine intolerance.

It's Partly About Self-Interest!

A confession: part of the reason for writing this book is self-interest. I, too, suffer from histamine intolerance and I find it so hard to find the right information on what I can, and cannot eat. There's actually a good reason for that. One important thing to point out straightaway is that no two people are the same when it comes to histamine symptoms, and what specifically causes a flare-up.

A Unique Approach to Low Histamine Recipes

So I looked at the other low-histamine cookbooks (with all respect, there aren't many and the choice isn't great), and decided on a special approach. I think it makes this the easiest histamine intolerance cookbook to use in the world. Well, at least out of the ones I've seen. In this book, I've consulted the most respected diet lists worldwide to create recipes, and I've collaborated with some of the best low-histamine cooks around. And labeled every ingredient, (which by the way took ages!).

References and Principle Sources for Histamine Diet Information

I've listed the histamine content of each ingredient on every single recipe throughout the book. You'll find the ingredients to be low-histamine (L), medium-histamine (M), or high-histamine (H). I'm proud of this approach and hope it makes it as simple as possible to eat healthily.

Introduction

In fact, I wish there were other decent low-histamine cookbooks out there that did the same thing.

The principle source is the food list over on my website, The Histamine Intolerance Site (www.histamineintolerance.net). As with all things histamine intolerance, opinions differ on histamine levels in food as well as histamine impact on the body of foods so I often consult other respected sources. Those include the 'SIGHI' Swiss Interest Group Histamine Intolerance list. It is a very well respected site which many Histamine Intolerant individuals consult daily and I urge you to have a look. Beth O'Hara's Mast Cell 360 Low Histamine Diet List is a fantastic resource that I have used, as well as, over the years, many others. In fact, I've approached many of the world's top histamine experts to come on my podcast Zestology over the years, and deeply appreciate their knowledge and contribution to helping us all feel better.

So to summarize, the best possible information available has been consulted to come up with the Histamine Food List.

But again, everyone is different. For some people this book will have listed ingredients that are low-histamine and they may end up causing you symptoms, however slight. I urge you to go carefully and try ingredients slowly, and always consult your practitioner. If, for instance, you react to onions but this book listed onions as low-histamine in this book, please make a note, as everyone reacts differently to different foods. That is part of the motivation behind this book - it really is hard to find the right information about histamine intolerance.

The wonderful thing is, once you start to follow the recipes in this cookbook and to use some of the supplements and lifestyle practices over in my Histamine Intolerance Explained book, your histamine bucket will start to reduce. You can even start to introduce foods that previously weren't possible. So, don't feel disheartened. Not only have you got over 70 delicious recipes in this book that are low-histamine, you will, hopefully, soon be able to re-introduce avocado and chocolate; although red wine might be a step too far – at least for me it is!

One of the Great Pleasures of Life

Food is one of the great pleasures in life. One of the problems with histamine intolerance and histamine intolerance diet lists is that you can sometimes end up avoiding so much of what makes us happy. That's why The Histamine Intolerance Cookbook wants to celebrate the finer things in life; come up with delicious recipes that leave you nourished, satisfied, and happy to eat on your own or share with friends. The other guiding force with this Histamine Intolerance Cookbook is that I didn't just want to make recipes that are low in histamine; I also wanted to create recipes that are healthy, nourishing and also fun – remember to look out for the Secret Sauces section!

I believe that a diet high in sugar, processed food and carbs can sometimes be unhealthy, but the problem is that often sugar and carbs can be low-histamine and therefore easy food choices. So, not only have I created the low-histamine cookbook with low-histamine recipes, you will also find that they are recipes that will nourish you and be healthy.

For instance, rather than sugar, recipes tend to use stevia – low-histamine (as long as you use it in powdered natural

Introduction

form rather than liquid form). I also never use microwaves and in fact we threw our microwave out - though I won't judge you if you keep yours. It's just I believe in making food the fresh and histamine-healthy way. In addition, I like using cassava flour (or other flours including rice flour) rather than normal flour. So those are just three of the ways in which I've introduced healthy recipes. In my own histamine intolerance journey, I have certainly found that lowering carbs has been quite helpful. Incidentally, I've also tried ketosis (ultra-low-carb dieting) to help with histamine intolerance symptoms. You can read more of the, er, mixed results, on that particular journey in the other book, Histamine Intolerance Explained, as there is a sizeable section on ketosis.

I've also drawn on primal cooking principles found in books such as Dave Asprey's Bulletproof Diet; prioritising fresh, healthy, grass-fed and the best ingredients on your body, as well as organic, super-fresh meat. Having presented the Zestology podcast for years, I noticed how these simple, primal dietary principles came up again and again for healthy living.

As you'll see I've marked the low-histamine meats on the list as being organic. If you want to eat meat, I think this is particularly important – grass-fed, pasture-raised happy animals provide better quality meat and will make you feel tons better. There is evidence to suggest this good quality meat is better for your histamine levels too, as well as being without the antibiotics, additives and stress hormones found in cheaper cuts. Finally, it's way better for the environment and karma to have good quality meat, so if you can afford organic meat, go for it. Otherwise, prioritize the highest quality meat you can afford.

But for now, enjoy the recipes and remember - every single ingredient in every single recipe is labeled according to the histamine intolerance food list: Low, Medium, or High Histamine. I do think that's really important, as I've read the other histamine intolerance cookbooks where all sorts of rather random ingredients pop up. I've used what I believe to be the best information possible to come up with this list. However, I realize there is always room for improvement; so, if you think that I've got an ingredient wrong please contact me at https://histamineintolerance.net/contact and I'll look into it. I'm a journalist who's enjoyed applying my skills to investigating this condition, and I'm happy to learn from you.

Finally, always check with your doctor or health practitioner before starting any new diet and following any of the recipes in this book. This cookbook is not advice; it is intended for information and discussion only. When it comes to histamine intolerance, it really does require the help of a skilled professional.

What Is Histamine Intolerance?

If you are reading this you probably have some idea that you might be suffering from histamine intolerance in some form. Histamine is actually very important to the human body. It's a chemical that is produced by the body to support a number of systems among which include: the central nervous system, the digestive system, and the immune system.

One of the best metaphors I've read on histamine came from the website WebMD. "Histamines act like bouncers at a club. They help your body get rid of something that's bothering you -- in this case, an allergy trigger, or "allergen."

When too much histamine builds in our bodies, there are too many "bouncers", all looking for troublemakers. That's when you can start to get adverse reactions and symptoms, and it can turn into histamine intolerance. This is a simplified explanation and there's plenty more detail in the other book, Histamine Intolerance Explained. Please feel free to consult that if you'd like more in-depth on the condition.

Why Follow A Low-Histamine Diet?

The whole point of this book is to show people living with histamine intolerance how to maintain optimum histamine blood levels through diet and without feeling the need to overly rely on over the counter or prescription medications.

When you get the low histamine diet right, your histamine intolerance symptoms will slowly (and sometimes very quickly) diminish. It's hugely satisfying, especially when you can eat deliciously (is that a word?) at the same time.

For the average person, it is tough to work out the amount of histamine found in food. It makes life a histamine guessing game for us lot!

As discussed in the Histamine Intolerance Explained title, certain food groups are known to have high histamine content. This is covered this in the other book but I'll list them once again for your reference.

Foods High in Histamine

- Fermented foods and beverages, including alcoholic drinks (red wine the worst.)
- Cured meats
- Soured foods
- Smoked foods

Why Follow A Low-Histamine Diet?

- Dried fruits
- Most fish (should only be fresh from the water or frozen within an hour – yes, I know this is unlikely, but unfortunately the bacteria level in fish goes up very quickly. Seek out companies like SeaFresh in the UK for amazing 'frozen-at-sea fish)
- Most citrus fruit
- Some nuts
- Aged cheese (young soft cheese normally okay)
- Leftovers (unless frozen straightaway, then should be okay)

Foods That Inhibit Effectiveness of Histamine-Regulating Enzymes

- Alcohol
- Avocado
- Chocolate (!)
- Cow's milk
- Bananas
- Some nuts
- Pineapple
- Papaya (I've found this particularly lethal)
- Strawberries
- Shellfish
- Tomatoes (difficult as occurs in a lot of recipes)
- Most artificial preservatives

With all this in mind, let's progress to the Low-Histamine Food List.

The Low-Histamine Food List

DISCLAIMER: Always check with your doctor or health practitioner before starting any new diet. This list is not advice; it is intended for information and discussion only. Histamine intolerance is extremely individual. Once again, always check with your doctor or health practitioner before starting any new diet or introducing any new food.

Low-Histamine Foods

- Acerola
- Amaranth
- Apricot
- Asparagus
- Beetroot
- Bison (organic, freshly cooked)
- Black caraway oil
- Blackcurrants
- Bok choi
- Broccoli
- Cabbage, green or white
- Cardamom
- Cauliflower
- Celery cabbage
- Cherry
- Agave syrup
- Apple
- Artichoke
- Basil
- Bell pepper (sweet)
- Black caraway
- Blackberry
- Blueberries
- Brazil nuts
- Butter
- Caraway
- Carrot
- Celery
- Chamomile tea
- Chestnut, sweet chestnut

The Low-Histamine Food List

- Chia
- Chicken (organic, freshly cooked)
- Chicory
- Cloves
- Coconut fat, oil
- Coconut, milk
- Common sea-buckthorn
- Coriander
- Corn salad, lamb's lettuce
- Cornflakes (if no additives)
- Courgette (zucchini)
- Cowberry
- Cranberry
- Cranberry nectar
- Cream, no additives
- Cucumber
- Dextrose
- Distilled white vinegar (nb other vinegars higher)
- Dragon fruit, pitaya
- Duck (organic, freshly cooked)
- Earth almond
- Elderflower cordial
- Endive
- Ewe's milk
- Farmer's cheese
- Fennel
- Flaxseed (also known as linseed)
- Fish, caught within 1 hour
- Fructose
- Garlic
- Geheimrats cheese
- Ginger
- Glucose
- Goat's milk
- Goji berry
- Goose (organic, freshly cooked)
- Gooseberries
- Gourds
- Grapes
- Hemp seeds
- Honey
- Inverted syrup
- Ispaghula
- Jostaberry
- Juniper berries
- Kaki
- Khorsan wheat
- Lactose
- Lamb (organic, freshly cooked)
- Lamb's lettuce

Histamine Intolerance Cookbook

- Lard
- Lime blossom tea
- Lychee
- Maltose
- Marrow
- Meridian fennel
- Millet
- Mint
- Morello cherries
- Nectarine
- Nigella sativa seed
- Oats
- Onions
- Ostrich (organic, freshly cooked)
- Palm kernel oil
- Palm sugar
- Parsley
- Peach
- Peppermint tea
- Persimmon
- Pomegranate
- Potato
- Psyllium
- Quail (organic, freshly cooked)
- Quince
- Rabbit (organic, freshly cooked)
- Raisins (no Sulphur)
- Rapeseed oil
- Lettuce
- Lingonberry
- Maltodextrin
- Maple syrup
- Melons (not watermelon)
- Milk, pasteurized or UHT
- Mineral water
- Monosodium ascorbate
- Napa cabbage
- Nigella sativa oil
- Nut grass
- Olive oil
- Oregano
- Pak choi
- Palm oil
- Paprika, sweet
- Parsnip
- Pearl sago
- Persian cumin
- Pitaya
- Pork (organic, freshly cooked)
- Poultry meat
- Pumpkins
- Quark
- Quinoa
- Radish
- Raw milk
- Redcurrants

The Low-Histamine Food List

Red cabbage
Rice
Roman coriander
Rosemary
Sage
Sago
Shallots
Sour cherry
Spirit vinegar
Starch
Sucrose
Sweetcorn
Tap water
Tiger nut sedge

Trout
Turmeric
Verbena tea
Wild rice

Rice noodles
Rooibos tea
Safflower oil
Sage tea
Sallow thorn
Sharon fruit
Spelt
Squashes
Stevia
Sugar
Sweet potato
Thyme
Tongue (veal, beef)
Turkey (organic, freshly cooked)
Veal, fresh
Whey
Yam
Zucchini (Courgette)

Medium-Histamine Foods

Almonds
Bamboo shoots
Barley
Beef (depending on age of beef, organic, freshly cooked)
Bread
Brussels sprouts

Anise, Aniseed
Barbay fig
Bay laurel, laurel
Boysenberry

Broad-leaved garlic
Buckrams

Histamine Intolerance Cookbook

- Cactus pear
- Chard stalks
- Chives
- Choko
- Cinnamon
- Cocoa butter
- Coke
- Cream cheese, plain
- Curd cheese
- Dates, dried
- Dog rose
- Egg yolk (different lists vary wildly with eggs so do test carefully, sometimes yolk thought to be better than white)
- Feta cheese
- Game
- German turnip
- Green beans
- Green split peas
- Hazelnut
- Horseradish
- Kohlrabi
- Laurel
- Lemonade
- Macadamia
- Cashew nuts
- Chayote
- Chokeberries
- Cilantro
- Coca-Cola
- Coffee (a contentious one – see more below)
- Cola-drinks
- Cress, garden cress
- Curry
- Dill
- Egg white (different lists vary wildly so do test carefully – more on eggs later on)
- Espresso
- Figs
- Garden cress
- Gouda, young
- Green peas
- Green tea
- Herbal teas
- Indian fig
- Ladyfinger banana
- Leek
- Loganberry
- Mango

The Low-Histamine Food List

Mascarpone cheese
Milk, lactose-free
Mozzarella
Mung beans
Nashi pear
Nuts
Olives
Pea shoots
Pistachio
Poppy seeds
Prickly pear
Purple granadilla
Ramsons
Ricotta cheese
Rose hip
Savoy cabbage
Snow peas
Sour cream
Star anise
Sugar banana
Tamarillo
Vanilla (extract, pod)
Vinegar (apple cider, white)
Wheat
White onion
Wild meat
Yeast
Yogurt, natural
Mate tea
Milk powder
Mulberry
Mushrooms
Nutmeg
Oat drinks
Paw paw
Pine nuts
Plum
Pear
Prune
Quinine
Rhubarb
Roquefort cheese
Rye
Sesame
Soft drinks
Spineless cactus
Stinging nettle tea
Sunflower oil
Turnip
Venison
Watermelon
White button mushroom
Wild garlic
Wood garlic
Yellow split peas
Zwetschge

High-Histamine Foods

Alcohol (unfortunately)
Alcoholic beverages
Algae and algae derivatives
Anchovies
Artificial sweeteners (always avoid!)
Aubergine
Avocado
Banana
Barley malt, malt
Beans (pulses)
Beer
Bell pepper (hot)
Bivalves (mussels, oyster, clams, scallops)
Blue cheese, mold cheese
Blue fenugreek
Borlotti beans
Bouillon
Brandy
Brown algae, algae
Buckwheat
Buttermilk (sour)
Cep
Champagne
Cheddar
Cheese (unpasteurized milk)
Cheese (hard, matured)
Chickpeas
Chili pepper, red
Chocolate drinks
Chufa sedge, roasted
Citrus fruits
Clover
Cocoa drinks
Cocoa
Crab
Crawfish
Crayfish
Cumin
Dried meat
Dry-cured ham
Eggplant
Energy drinks
Entrails
Ethanol
Extract of malt
Fenugreek
Fish, on ice
Fontina cheese
Gouda
Grapefruit
Green algae
Guava
Ham
Innards

The Low-Histamine Food List

- Jeera
- Kelp
- Kombu seaweed
- Lemon
- Lime
- Liquorice root
- Malt
- Margarine
- Mold cheese
- Mustard
- Orange
- Papaya
- Peanuts
- Perennial wall-rocket
- Pineapple
- Prawn
- Pulses (soy & peas)
- Red algae
- Rochefort cheese
- Rum
- Sauerkraut
- Schnapps
- Seaweed
- Shrimp
- Smoked meat
- Sparkling wine
- Spiny lobsters
- Stinging nettle
- Sunflower seeds
- Tomato
- Kefir
- Kiwi fruit
- Langouste
- Lentils
- Liquor
- Lobster
- Mandarin orange
- Meat
- Morel
- Nori seaweed
- Oyster
- Paprika, hot
- Pepper
- Pickled vegetables
- Porcini mushroom
- Processed cheese
- Raclette cheese
- Red wine
- Rock lobsters
- Salami
- Sausages, all
- Seafood, all
- Shellfish
- Smoked fish
- Soy products
- Spinach
- Spirits
- Strawberry
- Tea, black
- Trifolium

Trigonella
Vicia faba

Wakame seaweed
Wheat germ
Yeast extract

Tuna
Vinegar (balsamic, white wine)
Walnut
Wine

So that's the food list. As a reminder, going through the recipes, I've listed the histamine content of each ingredient on every single recipe throughout the book. You'll find the ingredients tend to be low-histamine (L), medium-histamine (M), or high-histamine (H) based on the best knowledge around. As always though, histamine intolerance is very individual so test new foods carefully.

A Quick Note on Coffee

So many people love coffee and find it haaaard to give up. My page on coffee on the website is one of the most visited, as a number of respected lists do list coffee as potentially high-histamine or histamine releasing. In addition, on some of the histamine intolerance forums, coffee is something that some people seem to struggle with. If you would love to carry on drinking coffee on your low-histamine diet, here are some things, which help;

1. Drink organic coffee and low mold coffee where possible. My current favourite is Exhale Coffee in the UK, plus Mindful Coffee in the States and Bulletproof Coffee, also USA-based.
2. Weird as it may sound, don't leave your coffee lying around for a long time before drinking it. Apart from the fact it'll be tepid when you drink it (never

The Low-Histamine Food List

ideal), some say this gives the coffee the chance to acquire more bacteria/histamine as it sits.

It's not strictly a recipe, but coffee is important so I wanted to address it here. There is more on my site at:

https://histamineintolerance.net/blog/histamine-and-coffee.

Now on with the recipes.

BREAKFAST RECIPES

Apple and Pumpkin Seed Granola

A delicious start to my low histamine recipes – the baking is where the magic happens. The flaked almonds go really well with this, but remember you always have the flaxseed option if almonds don't agree with you.

Serves 1-2 medium bowl

Ingredients:

- 1 cup gluten-free oats, jumbo or regular (L)
- 1 red apple, large gratings (L)
- 1 tbsp. pumpkin seeds (L)
- OPTIONAL: ½ tsp. cinnamon (M)
- 1 serving stevia (L)
- 2 tsp. coconut oil (L)
- OPTIONAL: 1 tbsp. flaked almonds (M)

Instructions:

1. Preheat oven to 175°C and prepare a baking sheet.
2. In a bowl, mix the grated apple with all the dry ingredients.
3. In a saucepan, heat up the wet ingredients (coconut oil and stevia) until they dissolve.
4. Combine both mixtures and stir to coat well.
5. Spread evenly onto the baking sheet and let it bake for about 25 minutes until golden brown. Stir every 10 minutes. Keep an eye on it after 15 minutes for any signs of burning - it can turn quickly!
6. Let the granola cool and serve or store in an air-tight container.

Carrot Cake Porridge

Yum. This recipe is lovely, and particularly nice with some histamine-lowering apple on top. Go easy on the stevia, as it's often very sweet, even more so than sugar. But it's a healthier, natural choice if you require a little extra sweetness. More on natural sweeteners as we go. Enjoy!

Please note – I've used coconut milk in this and many of the recipes, but it can be interchangeable with other non-dairy milks (or mylks to use the trendy term) depending on your own low-histamine preferences. Try to find one without fillers, some people say they react to certain ingredients in commercial coconut milk brands including guar gum.

Serves 1 medium bowl

Ingredients:

- ½ cup gluten-free oats (L)
- ½ carrot, grated (L)
- Stevia, to taste or 1 tbsp. raw honey (L)
- 1 tbsp. pumpkin seeds (L)
- 1 cup coconut milk (L)
- OPTIONAL: 1 tsp. cinnamon (M)
- Optional Toppings: apple or pear pieces (L)

Instructions:

1. In a saucepan, cook carrots, coconut milk, and oats over medium heat for about 8 minutes; stirring frequently.
2. Add or reduce coconut milk to your desired consistency.

3. Serve into a bowl, drizzle with stevia or honey and finish with your preferred toppings. NB, pumpkin seeds are low histamine on the most respected lists, but I am aware that some people find these to be problematic. In fact, I tend to indulge only occasionally myself. As always, follow my mantra and test, test again. You'll see pumpkin seeds pop up a lot as many seem to be fine on them, but just remember - everybody reacts differently.

Maple Coconut Granola

This is an excellent recipe, and a nice breakfast option for us low-histamine folk. I am willing to bet that your granola doesn't last very long after cooking, and may get raided throughout the day. You'll notice there are a few options, that's because you can mix and match your favourite ingredients.

Serves 4 small bowls

Ingredients:

- 2 cups gluten-free oats (L)
- 3 tbsp. pumpkin seeds (L)
- 3 tbsp. coconut flakes (L)
- 3 tbsp. MCT oil or coconut oil (L)
- ¼ cup maple syrup (L)
- OPTIONAL: 1 tsp. cinnamon (M)
- OPTIONAL: 3 tbsp. flaked almonds (M)
- OPTIONAL: A little ginger (L)

Instructions:

1. Preheat your oven to 150°C (approx 300°F) and prepare a baking sheet.
2. In one bowl, mix all the dry ingredients together except the coconut flakes.
3. Melt the coconut oil, and then add to a bowl with your maple syrup.

4. Combine these two mixtures and stir thoroughly to coat well.
5. Spread the combined mixture onto the baking sheet and bake for 15 to 20 minutes; stirring halfway through the baking process.
6. Remove from the oven once it turns light golden brown and let the granola cool down. Sprinkle over your coconut flakes.
7. Store in an air tight container or serve immediately.

Breakfast Blackberry and Chia Pudding

Chia seeds are versatile ingredients, and very filling. The Bulletproof Diet does list chia seeds as being only mid-range in terms of inflammation, though I find them absolutely fine. I have been lucky enough to speak to Alzheimer's expert and NYT bestselling author Dr. Dale Bredesen on my podcast Zestology a number of times. I asked him about the particular problem of histamine and Omega 3s and he recommended chia as another source. So here we go.

Serves 1 large smoothie glass.

Ingredients:

- 2 tbsp. chia seeds (L)
- 1 cup milk, non-dairy (L)
- 1 tsp. Monk Fruit sweetener or small tbsp. of honey (L)
- ¾ cup fresh blackberries (L)
- 1 tbsp. pumpkin seeds (L)

Instructions:

1. Gently heat the blackberries in a saucepan for 4-5 minutes so that they soften and release their juices.
2. Once the blackberries have cooled transfer this and all the other ingredients into a mason jar.

3. Stir well and cover with an air-tight lid. Let it sit in the fridge for a couple of hours. Let the chia seeds expand.
4. Add coconut milk if you wish to thin the pudding's consistency, or play around with flavours and textures.
5. Serve immediately.

Butter Coffee with Rosemary

What's coffee doing in the breakfast section? What's butter doing in coffee? What's rosemary got to do with anything? So many questions here.

Intermittent fasting has helped many in the low histamine community and you might want to try it. It means compressing your meals into a 'feeding window' and gives your body time to rest from digestion. Butter Coffee - made popular by Bulletproof - can help with this and can provide a filling, high-fat but healthy start to the day that won't spike your blood sugar. Some people love it, some people can't get their heads round it, I say give it a go, even if it ends up being an occasional treat.

Huge thanks to my friend and popular instagrammer Ryan Carter (@livevitae on insta) who provides the inspiration for this Bulletproof Coffee twist with the genius addition of rosemary. Butter and coffee are listed as (M) in my food list so test carefully., but this is one recipe that works fine for me and many others. There's more on coffee and histamine in the Low Histamine Food List section.

Serves 1.

Ingredients:

- Ground organic coffee (M)
- 1 tbsp MCT Oil (L)
- 1 tbsp butter or ghee (M)

- Few sprigs of rosemary (L)

Instructions:

1. Make your coffee with a french press.
2. Drop the sprigs of rosemary into the french press. The hot water releases all the polyphenol histamine-lowering essential-oil goodness of the rosemary.
3. Once your rosemary coffee infusion is ready, take out the sprigs, add the MCT Oil and butter and blend.

Maple Cherry Chia Pudding

Fun and fruity, and perfect for an easy breakfast. You can always sprinkle some granola on top too. Adjust the sweetness of the pudding by adding maple syrup to your taste preference, though remember I prioritize a lower sugar, lower carb diet to heal the gut.

Serves 1

Ingredients:

- 2 tbsp. chia seeds (L)
- ¾ cup cherries (L)
- ½ cup milk, non-dairy (L)
- 1 tsp. maple syrup (L)
- 1 tbsp. pumpkin seeds as a topping (L)

Instructions:

1. Halve the cherries and then gently heat in a saucepan on a low heat for 4-5 minutes so they release their juices.
2. Add the chia seeds and milk to a mason jar along with the cherries once cooled. Stir very thoroughly.
3. Refrigerate the chia pudding for several hours, giving them a stir halfway through.
4. If you need to, add a little more milk for a thinner consistency, and serve immediately.

Blueberry Quinoa Bake

Oh good. A chance to get stuck into a favourite ingredient - flaxseed (sometimes known as linseed). People with histamine intolerance can react variably to different nuts and seeds, but I've found ground flaxseed to be one of the most absolute reliable in terms of making me feel good. They work great in this recipe, but feel free to go flaxseed crazy and keep a bag at all times for smoothies, salads, desserts (it makes a good substitute cheesecake base). I like to pay a little extra and buy sprouted flaxseed for extra digestibility and deliciousness. If you do this, keep the bag in the fridge once open.

Serves 4 bowls

Ingredients:

FOR THE BAKE:
- 1 cup quinoa uncooked (L)
- 1 cup coconut milk (L)
- 2 cups fresh blueberries (L)
- 2 tbsp. ground flaxseeds (sprouted if you can find them) (L)
- 6 tbsp. water (L)
- Stevia, to taste or 2 tbsp. honey (L)

FOR THE TOPPINGS:
- 1 tbsp. pumpkin seeds (L)
- 1 tbsp. fresh blueberries (L)
- OPTIONAL: 1 tbsp. flaked almonds (M)
- 1 tbsp. honey (optional) (L)

Blueberry Quinoa Bake

Instructions:

1. Preheat oven to 175°C (350°F) and prepare a baking dish.
2. Meanwhile, mix flaxseeds and some water and set aside to combine.
3. Into a baking dish, combine all the ingredients of the bake and stir well. Don't forget the flaxseeds.
4. Bake for about one hour; stirring half-way through.
5. When done, set aside to cool.
6. Add your preferred toppings and enjoy!

Vegetarian Granola Breakfast Pizza

Breakfast Pizza sounds so wrong doesn't it. But trust me, this recipe works and is surprisingly delicious with some fruit or a little coconut cream. How could you refuse this for a decadent, delicious start to the day?

Vegetarian Granola Breakfast Pizza

Serves 2 (one half is one serving)

Ingredients:

- 2 tbsp. flaxseeds (L)
- 2 tbsp. sesame seeds (L)
- 2 tbsp. chia seeds (L)
- 1 cup oats (L)
- Stevia, to taste or 1/2 tbsp. honey (L)
- 2 tbsp. pumpkin seed butter (L)
- 1 tsp. olive oil (L)
- 1 tsp. butter (L)
- OPTIONAL: 1 tsp. cinnamon (M)
- TOPPINGS: blueberries (L), coconut cream (L)

Instructions:

1. Preheat oven to 170°C and prepare a baking sheet.
2. In a small bowl, soak the seeds in ½ cup of water for 10-20 mins.
3. In a separate bowl, mix the pumpkin seed butter, oats, honey, cinnamon, and olive oil. Add the soaked seeds into the mixture and stir well.
4. Spread out the mixture into a pizza shape onto the baking sheet.
5. Bake for about half an hour. (Edges should be golden brown).
6. Let it cool and add your preferred toppings. Enjoy!

Breakfast Granola with Coconut Cream

I love coconut – you might have realized that already - and use it in lots of different ways. This recipe combines coconut with oats. Oats didn't previously particularly excite me previously. But they are a reliable, low-histamine food that grow on me every day, and if you buy gluten-free you're guaranteed not to be contaminated with wheat. You'll find I really enjoy using them in my recipes – after all being histamine intolerant means being adaptable. It's the coconut cream that makes this special.

A note on oats: there are some widely available 'oat creams' available now. Check the ingredients carefully, one I looked at contained vegetable oil, a load of preservatives and a method of processing the oats which means they can have a higher GI than sugar. All of this won't help your health, and probably won't help your histamine intolerance. What have we learnt? Stick to simple single ingredient foods where possible, and check labelling. Most coconut creams have one ingredient and that'll do for me just fine.

Serves 1 bowl

Ingredients:

- 1 cup of the aforementioned oats (L)
- 3 tbsp. pumpkin seeds (L)
- Stevia, to taste or 2 tbsp. honey (L)
- 2 tbsp. olive oil (L)

Breakfast Granola with Coconut Cream

- 1 tbsp. desiccated coconut (L)
- OPTIONAL: ½ tsp. cinnamon (M)
- ¼ tsp. pink Himalayan salt (L)
- OPTIONAL: 3 tbsp. almonds (M – only if you don't react to them)
- Toppings: 2 tbsp. blueberries and/or 2 tbsp. organic coconut cream (L)

Instructions:

1. Preheat oven to 150°C and prepare a baking sheet.
2. In a medium bowl, combine the dry ingredients, except the coconut, and stir well.
3. Add all the wet ingredients into the bowl and mix well to coat.
4. Spread the mixture evenly onto the baking sheet and bake for 12-15 minutes stirring frequently.
5. Add the coconut and let it bake for a couple more minutes.
6. Oaty deliciousness awaits. Let it cool. Add your preferred toppings. Enjoy!

Sweet Potato and Corn Hash

Savory deliciousness. Makes good use of my delicious ketchup recipe which you'll find later in the book.

Serves 2 plates

Ingredients:

- 2 medium sweet potatoes, cut into bite-size pieces (L)
- 1 cup sweetcorn (L)
- ½ white onion, diced (L)
- 2 slices cauliflower bread, toasted (L) (see recipe below)
- 2 tsp. olive oil (L)
- 1 tsp. thyme (L)
- Salt, to taste (L)
- Fresh coriander (L)
- Butter (L)
- Low Histamine Ketchup (recipe in Secret Sauce section) (L)

Instructions:

1. Preheat oven to 200°C and prepare a baking sheet.
2. Spread out the sweet potato pieces onto the baking sheet and drizzle with olive oil and sprinkle with thyme.
3. Bake for 20-30 minutes. Let it cool. Separately fry the onions lightly in butter, then mix in sweetcorn to warm.

Sweet Potato and Corn Hash

4. Butter the bread slices and mix your ingredients together. Season to your liking and add the Low-Histamine Ketchup.
5. Garnish with coriander. Serve immediately.

CAULIFLOWER BREAD

The humble cauliflower, I salute you! This is absolutely delicious and a great way to incorporate all my favourite dietary principles. I like eating low histamine, but also relatively low sugar and healthily too, and sadly it's often hard to marry the two together. But this bread is the perfect, low-carb, low-histamine treat. I give a big shout out to Tania from the Histamine Friendly Kitchen for the inspiration for this one. Thanks Tania for letting me use this recipe and get all cauliflowery.

A note on eggs. I've read other histamine intolerance cookbooks where there are a lot of egg-based recipes, and I think that's a shame as I know that some people simply don't react well to them. I know tolerate eggs absolutely fine and love them. But... I've done a lot of healing, and you may not be there yet.

I've restricted this cookbook to very few eggs throughout and they are never a main ingredient. A good suggestion is to try substituting one egg for 3/4 quail eggs. In general quail eggs are tolerated better by many with histamine intolerance.

Serves: Makes 1 loaf

Ingredients:

- 1 cup cassava flour or brown rice flour or coconut flour (L)
- 1 tsp. salt (L)
- 1 tsp. baking powder (L)

Cauliflower Bread

- ½ cup frozen cauliflower (L)
- ¼ cup coconut milk (L)
- 2 tbsp. extra virgin olive oil (L)
- 1 egg (M)

Instructions:

1. Preheat oven to 200°C and prepare a baking sheet.
2. In a bowl, mix the dry ingredients and set aside.
3. In a blender, process the wet ingredients until smooth.
4. Add the wet mixture into the dry mixture and fold gently until a smooth dough forms.
5. Spoon the dough onto the baking sheet and sprinkle your preferred toppings.
6. Bake for about 20 minutes until it turns golden brown.
7. Let it cool and use as it as sandwich bread.

Blackberry, Oat and Coconut Smoothie

What's not to love about this smoothie? It's a beaut. I like to buy frozen organic fruit. Not only is it fresher (and therefore lower histamine), it's delicious whichever way you eat it, if more expensive to go organic. I just feel it is worth it for my health.

Serves 1: 240ml to 300ml

Ingredients:

- 1 cup cherries, pitted (L)
- ½ cup gluten-free oats (L)
- ½ cup blackberries (L)
- ½ cup coconut milk (L) + more, if needed
- 1 tbsp. coconut flakes (L)
- 1 tbsp. whey (L)
- Ice cubes (L)

Instructions:

1. With this smoothie, first transfer all the ingredients in a high-powered blender. With smoothies I use a NutriBullet which is quite affordable, but any brand will do as long as it can churn it up nice and quick.
2. Process until it is smooth or to your desired consistency. Add more milk if required.
3. Drink immediately. Well you won't be able to resist anyway.

Blueberry Breakfast Smoothie

Blueberries are better to buy organic due to the pesticides that can accumulate on the skin. So if you can pay a little extra, get some organic blueberries, put them in the freezer (my absolute fave) and pull out whenever you want a snack, or a blueberry and whey smoothie. So refreshing. On this and other recipes you'll see that I've put stevia/honey to taste if you have a sweet tooth. Stevia is a reliable natural sweetener, but ideally you want to be avoiding particularly sugary foods. The link between histamine intolerance and candida is fairly well established and the sugar can feed that candida. So go easy on the sweet treats, and give organic stevia, or even organic monk fruit sweetener a go ahead of honey and see if you enjoy.

Serves 2 glasses

Ingredients:

- 1 cup fresh blueberries (L)
- ½ cup fresh blackberries (L)
- 2 tbsp. whey protein powder (L) (go easy and test, use brown rice protein or pea protein if it suits you better)
- OPTIONAL: 1 tbsp. almond butter (M)
- 1 cup coconut milk or oat milk (L), more to preferred consistency.
- Stevia, to taste or 1 small tbsp. honey (L)

Instructions:

1. Transfer all the ingredients in a high-powered blender.
2. Process until it is smooth or to your desired consistency. Add water, if necessary.
3. Serve immediately

Melon, Peach and Chia Smoothie

So refreshing. The coconut milk makes this a tropical sun-kissed drink.

Almond butter appears in this recipe. I've changed my mind on almond butter a little since the first edition of this book. I love it, and that's the problem. I never seem to eat just a tiny bit. In the intervening years since original publication I'm thankfully a lot less sensitive, and eat a lot more foods. But almond butter is one thing I don't eat any more. In short, I kicked the habit!

But it's listed as (M) medium, and you might be okay with it. Test carefully.

Serves 1-2 glasses (depending on consistency)

Ingredients:

- ½ cantaloupe melon, diced (L)
- 1 peach, stone removed and cut into pieces (L)
- ¾ cup coconut milk (L)
- OPTIONAL: 2 tsp. almond butter (M)
- 1 tbsp. chia seeds (L)
- 1 very small tbsp. agave syrup but it's delicious on its own (L)
- Ice cubes (L)

Instructions:

1. Transfer all the ingredients in a high-powered blender.
2. Process until it is smooth or to your desired consistency.
3. Serve immediately.

Green Breakfast Power Smoothie

I find celery to be a wonder ingredient, histamine lowering, and surprisingly tasty on its own in a simple celery juice. If you'd rather keep it simple, just juice up a load of celery. Or keep the goodness in and make this smoothie with a bunch of other histamine-lowering ingredients. And pay attention to how you feel on celery, it makes me feel great. There are a few more celery-based dishes sprinkled throughout this book.

Serves 2 glasses

Ingredients:

- 1½ cup water or more to add consistency (L)
- 1 handful pea shoots (just for the extra histamine-lowering potential.) (L)
- 1 cup celery (L)
- 2 carrots, cleaned, peeled, and diced (L)
- 1 medium apple, sliced (L)
- 2 tsp. ginger, freshly grated (L)

Instructions:

1. Whack all the ingredients in your blender.
2. Whizz until smooth.
3. Drink.

Apple Pie Smoothie

Apple pie, tick. Smoothie, tick. Apple Pie Smoothie – sign me up. Don't be put off by the cauliflower in this recipe, it's a great way to get some extra nutritious cruciferous veggies into your diet, and it all adds to the fun. I'd like to say thank you again to the wonderful Tania from The Histamine Friendly Kitchen Blog for letting me get inspired by her version of this recipe. Do check her out, she's brilliant and her blog is full of yummy recipes.

Serves 2 glasses

Ingredients:

- 2 sweet apples (L)
- 1 cup frozen cauliflower (L)
- 4 tbsp. rolled gluten-free oats (L)
- OPTIONAL: 1 tsp. cinnamon (M)
- ½ tsp. ginger, freshly minced (L)
- 2 cups coconut milk (L)
- 1 tbsp. whey protein powder (L)
- OPTIONAL: 2 dates, dried (M)

Instructions:

1. You know the smoothie drill by now. Put in blender.
2. Blend.
3. Drink.
4. You are living the low-histamine dream.

Sweet Melon Smoothie

I used to make this recipe with coconut yogurt. But that was in simpler times when I didn't realize I had histamine intolerance. Now I do, my coconut yogurt addiction is a thing of the past, and surprise surprise, I feel soooo much better.

I still miss coconut yogurt and in fact over on the blog at The Histamine Intolerance Site, I've been experimenting with making my own. Call me sad, but it's quite an exciting process using histamine-intolerance-friendly bacteria only. It also involves using the Instant Pot mentioned elsewhere in this book.

Back to this recipe, and in truth it never needed coconut yogurt in the first place. But if you are a home-made yogurt maker, feel free to add your own.

Serves 1

Ingredients:

- 1 cup sweet melon, cube pieces (L)
- 2 tbsp. unsulphured raisins (L)
- 1 tbsp. ground flaxseed (L)
- 1 cup coconut milk (L)
- OPTIONAL SWEET TOOTH EXTRA: 3 dates (M)

Instructions:

1. Combine all ingredients in a high-speed blender. Raisins are sweet but a 0 on the SIGHI scale so I use them in small quantities for taste.
2. Process until very smooth.
3. Serve immediately in a glass. Enjoy!

"Hidden Health" Smoothie

There is so much goodness in this smoothie with the greens hiding in there and it still has just the right amount of sweetness with the blueberries and melon. If you can't source pea shoots feel free to substitute in other low-histamine greens. I told you I like blueberries and they're a great addition here. I always freeze them to preserve freshness, tastiness and low-histamineness.

Serves 2 glasses

Ingredients:

- 1 cup pea shoots (L)
- 5 baby carrots (L)
- ¼ cup blueberries (L)
- 1 to 1½ cup coconut milk (as always you can use other low-histamine milks) (L)
- 1 cup sweet melon chunks (or another low histamine fruit) (L)
- (Optional) 1 tbsp chia seeds to up your Omega 3 intake. (L)

Instructions:

1. Blend it all up.
2. Process until smooth.
3. Serve immediately in a glass. Enjoy!

Cherry Smoothie

This cherry smoothie is fun, fruity and has a secret ingredient! It uses a small amount of cauliflower to work as a thickener in place of banana, which is often used in smoothies. Serve this to the kids and they will have no idea they are also eating some vegetables!

Cherry Smoothie

Serves 2 small glasses

Ingredients:

- 1 cup cherries (fresh or frozen) (L)
- ½ cup blueberries (fresh or frozen) (L)
- ½ cup milk of your choice (L)
- ¼ cup cauliflower (frozen) (L)
- 1 tbsp. coconut flakes (L)
- Ice, to taste preference (L)

Instructions:

1. Add all the ingredients to a blender other than the ice.
2. Add ice gradually for the consistency that you prefer.
3. Serve immediately. Enjoy!

SNACKS RECIPES

BURGER BITES

This is one of my favorite recipes in the whole book. I often do a big batch of my Burger Bites, eat some fresh from the oven and then freeze the rest. It's so convenient to have Burger Bites when I need them. Lunch for me about three days a week is one or two of these with some butternut squash and a pea shoot salad drizzled with olive oil. Remember to make use of the freezer for your leftovers to minimize histamine accumulation, and enjoy these sensational Burger Bites.

There's been a big debate in the team about whether this is a 'snack' or a 'main course'. I've left it under 'Snacks' but simply increase the size a little when you make the patties to turn these burger bites into a main meat dish.

Note: The fresher the ground meat the better, as minced meat tends to accumulate more histamine. I even know some histamine intolerant people who have a meat grinder in their home! We have recently moved house and our local butcher has a meat grinder - and is happy to grind any meat on demand. Lovely. I use turkey mince here but this recipe also works great with pork and beef mince.

Serves 10 Burger Bites

Ingredients:

- 1 lb. fresh and lean turkey mince (L)
- ¼ cup coconut milk (L)
- ¼ cup parsley, chopped (L)

- 1 tsp. oregano (L)
- 2 cloves garlic, minced (L)
- ¼ cup white onion, diced (L)
- 1 tsp. sweet paprika (nb – sweet paprika is listed as low histamine, hot paprika is high histamine) (L)
- 1 tsp. fresh basil, chopped (L)
- 1 tsp. coriander, dried (L)
- 1 tsp. thyme (L)
- Salt, to taste (L)

Instructions:

1. Preheat oven to 200°C (400°F) and prepare a baking sheet.
2. In a large bowl, mix all ingredients together. Be careful not to overmix.
3. Form about 10 mini turkey patties with your hand. Arrange the patties in the sheet.
4. Bake for 30 to 40 minutes until cooked through. Serve with a side of vegetables.

Oven-Baked Apple Trail Mix

A versatile snack for when you are out and about. The seeds in this recipe are (L) in the list, but some of my followers find them higher in histamine so go carefully and test, as always.

Serves 1 medium bowl.

Ingredients:

- 2 apples, sliced (L)
- 1 cup pumpkin seeds (L)
- ¾ cup shredded coconut (L)
- Coconut oil (L)
- ¼ cup hemp seeds (L)
- OPTIONAL: ¼ cup flaked almonds (M)
- OPTIONAL: ½ cup pistachios non-salted (M)

Instructions:

1. Preheat oven to 160°C (320°F) and prepare a baking sheet. Lightly brush with melted coconut oil.
2. Transfer apple slices to the sheet and bake for 30-40 minutes; or until slightly crispy. Turn the apple slices halfway through cooking.
3. Remove the apple slices from oven and let them cool.
4. Combine everything in a bowl and toss well to mix.
5. Serve immediately.

Homemade Sweet Potato Chips

On all the forums and sites that I visit on Histamine Intolerance, sweet potatoes seem to be a reliable low histamine food (although some have to watch out for oxalates). So let's make some sweet potato chips. Yes, I know this recipe is super simple. But sometimes it's the simple ones that are the best. This book is all about nourishing food that helps you heal. If you really want to make these special, buy a baking sheet with tiny little holes in it. It'll make your sweet potato chips sing.

Serves 1 large bowl

Ingredients:

- 2 medium sweet potatoes, thinly sliced (L)
- 1 tbsp. extra-virgin olive oil (L)
- Salt to taste (L)

Instructions:

1. Preheat oven to 210°C (410°F) and line a baking sheet with foil.
2. Spread out the sweet potato pieces on the sheet. Do not stack them.
3. Brush with olive oil (must be extra virgin, this is an absolute staple in my low histamine kitchen). Either use a brush or get dirty with your hands and make sure they get a really good coating. Then

Homemade Sweet Potato Chips

bake until golden brown (25 minutes but keep an eye on them).
4. Remove from oven once they are starting to brown, season, and serve in a bowl. A simple recipe, yes, but a low-histamine one that is always reliable. And stand-by for more from The Sweet Potato Appreciation Society later on.

Maca Coconut Cream with Blueberries

Sometimes you're running late, the kids need feeding, you need to put a wash on, AND make yourself a quick low-histamine snack/breakfast before you get out the door. This might do the trick, and you can always mix in some of my histamine-friendly granola if needed.

So what's the maca bit all about? Native to South America, maca root is a caffeine-free, plant-based superfood containing a host of healing minerals. It is great for energy, wellness and even libido! It also has a caramelly, nutty flavour that's hard not to love. I tolerate it perfectly well and get an energy boost from it every time. However it is not listed on the SIGHI scale or on many food lists and so I have listed it as (M) for this recipe. The first time you try it go very carefully with it to test and let me know how you go with it so I can keep this cookbook and research updated. Do not use maca if pregnant or breastfeeding, and if in doubt always ask your doctor.

Serves 1 medium bowl

Ingredients:

- 1 cup coconut cream (L)
- ¼ cup coconut water (L)
- A small sprinkling of organic maca powder (M)
- A pinch of salt (L)
- Blueberries, for topping (L)

Maca Coconut Cream with Blueberries

Instructions:

1. In a blender, process coconut cream, coconut water, maca and salt until well mixed.
2. Serve in a bowl and top with blueberries.

Herbed Oat Crackers

These herbed oat crackers are a perfect snack for you or the kids, and so easy to make. With lots of oats, seeds and herbs they are full of healthy ingredients. If you like an extra 'herby' taste then add a little more of your favourite herb. These fun, chewy crackers are great with any low histamine cheese, jam or on their own with a salad or soup. Best eaten on the day they are made.

Herbed Oat Crackers

Makes 6 small crackers (approx. 8x6 cm.)

Ingredients:

- ¾ cup oats (L)
- ¼ cup pumpkin seeds (L)
- 1 tbsp. chia seeds (L)
- ½ tbsp. flax seeds (L)
- 1 tbsp. sesame seeds (M)
- 1 tbsp. maple syrup (more to taste) (L)
- ½ cup water (L)
- ½ tsp. dried thyme (L)
- ½ tsp. dried oregano (L)
- ½ tsp. dried basil (L)

Instructions:

1. Preheat the oven to 180C and line a baking tray with parchment paper.
2. Add all the ingredients to a bowl and stir really well so it's combined. If it looks too dry, then add a touch more water. Cover and leave to sit for at least ten minutes.
3. Spread the mixture on your baking tray, into an even layer. If there is any excess water try not to include this. The oat mixture should be about 0.5cm thick.
4. Bake for 25 minutes, but watch for any signs of the edges burning.
5. Remove from the oven, flip (carefully!) and bake for a further 10-15 minutes.
6. Leave to cool and then top with your favourite low histamine spread!

Pumpkin Seed Butter

This pumpkin seed butter is delicious and has a healthy helping of good fats, and it's always important to get enough of them. As I said earlier, test pumpkin seeds cautiously, as some people have a reaction to them.

Pumpkin Seed Butter

Serves 1 cup

Ingredients:

- 1 cup pumpkin seeds (L)
- 2 tbsp. coconut oil, food grade (L)
- OPTIONAL: 1 tsp. cinnamon (M)

Instructions:

1. Preheat the oven to 160°C and prepare a baking sheet.
2. Transfer the pumpkin seeds on the sheet evenly and bake until they start to pop (about 13 minutes).
3. Transfer the seeds into a blender and pulse blend until a smooth butter forms. You will likely have to scrape the sides of the blender down a few times. Set aside.
4. Heat the coconut oil in a pan until it turns to liquid.
5. Add the coconut oil mixture into the pumpkin seed butter, sprinkle over the cinnamon, if using, and stir well to combine.
6. Serve with a side of fruit. Or on it's own.

SOUP RECIPES

Butternut Squash and Turmeric Soup

This is a simple but very tasty soup that is brimming with healthy nutrients - and look at that color. This soup has a touch of maple syrup for a bit of sweetness, so have a try if you have a sweet tooth, but feel free to leave out if you prefer.

Serves 2

Ingredients:

- ¼ white onion (L)
- 1 garlic clove, minced (L)
- 2 cups butternut squash (L)
- 1 cup carrots (L)
- ½ red bell pepper (L)
- 2 cups vegetable stock (L)
- ½ tsp. turmeric (L)
- ½ cm. ginger (L)
- ½ tsp. maple syrup (optional) (L)
- salt, to taste (L)
- 1 tbsp. pumpkin seeds (L)

Instructions:

1. Fry the onion and garlic on a low heat for 3-4 minutes until softened, and then add in the vegetables, turmeric and ginger. Cook for 5-6 minutes.
2. Pour in your vegetable stock and bring to the boil. Reduce the heat and cook on a light simmer for 20 minutes.
3. Add the salt, and maple syrup if using.
4. Transfer to a blender and process until smooth.
5. Sprinkle on the pumpkin seeds, and serve warm into your bowls.

Wild Rice Vegetable Soup

Hearty and delicious, this will fill you up anytime. The recipe makes two big portions so if you can't eat it all, either share a bowl or store in the freezer for another time in a silicon bag. Remember to never store leftovers. Unfortunately it's just not good for us histamine folk, although your other family members might want to get involved if they don't have histamine issues.

Serves 2 large bowls

Ingredients:

- ½ cup wild rice (L) (you could also use black rice, which is absolutely delicious, but takes about 40 minutes to cook).
- 3 small-medium carrots, chopped (L)
- 1 small zucchini, chopped (L)
- 1 small squash, chopped (L)
- ½ cup Asian cabbage or Chinese leaf cabbage, chopped (L)
- 1 tsp. dried thyme (L)
- 1 tsp. dried basil (L)
- 2 tsp. sweet paprika (L)
- 2 cups vegetable stock (L)
- ½ cup coconut milk (L)
- Fresh parsley, for garnish (L)
- 1 tbsp. olive oil (L)
- 3 cups water (L)

Instructions:

1. Heat the oil in a large saucepan and sauté the vegetables for about 5 minutes.
2. Add the herbs into the pan along with the wild rice.
3. Pour vegetable stock into the pan and stir well. Bring to a boil and then let it simmer for about 20 minutes. Stir occasionally. Pour in the coconut milk after returning the soup to a simmer.
4. You can add water to achieve your desired consistency.
5. Serve while warm into a bowl and garnish with fresh parsley.

Sweet Potato Quinoa Soup

A hearty lunch or light dinner, this sweet potato quinoa soup is really healthy with all the vegetables and has plant-based protein from the quinoa. You can always swap vegetables in and out for your favorite ones. The optional coconut milk makes it creamy, but it's good without too.

Serves 2

Ingredients:

- 1 tbsp. olive oil (L)
- ½ white onion, diced (L)
- 1 cup broccoli, diced (L)
- 1 carrot, diced (L)
- 1 small sweet potato, diced (L)
- 1 cup butternut squash, diced (L)
- 60g quinoa, rinsed (L)
- 3 cups vegetable stock + more to preferred consistency (L)
- 1 tsp. turmeric (L)
- 1 tsp. sweet paprika (L)
- 1 tsp. thyme (L)
- pinch, salt (L)
- OPTIONAL: 1 cup coconut milk (L)

Instructions:

1. In a large saucepan gently fry the onion in olive oil for 4-5 minutes until softened. Then sprinkle in the herbs and spices.

2. Add the quinoa, vegetables and vegetable stock, give it a good stir and bring to the boil. Reduce the heat to a very low simmer, add the coconut milk if using, and cook for 20-25 minutes until the quinoa has 'opened' and the vegetables are cooked through.
3. Sprinkle on the salt, and serve up in your bowls. Serve immediately and enjoy.

Classic Pumpkin Soup

Serves 2 large bowls

Ingredients:

- 1 tbsp. olive oil (L)
- 4-5 cups pumpkin peeled and diced (L)
- 1 tbsp. cloves (L)
- ½ white onion, diced (L)
- 2 carrots, diced (L)
- ½ cup coconut milk (L)
- 3 cups vegetable stock (L)
- 1 tsp. turmeric (L)
- 1 tsp. sweet paprika (L)
- 1 tsp. thyme (L)

TOPPINGS:
- 1 tbsp. pumpkin seeds (L)
- 1 slice cauliflower bread, cut into cubes (L)
- 2 tsp. olive oil (L)
- Salt, to taste (L)

Instructions:

1. Sauté the onions in a large saucepan for about 4 minutes and then stir in the herbs and spices.
2. Stir in the pumpkin pieces and carrot, and continue cooking for 12 minutes.
3. Add the vegetable stock and coconut milk, bring to a boil and then let it simmer for another 12 minutes.
4. Meanwhile, sauté bread and pumpkin seeds until they become crispy to make croutons.
5. Transfer the pumpkin soup mixture into a blender and process until very smooth.
6. Serve warm into a bowl and top with croutons and other toppings.

Sumptuous Celery Soup

Celery is a wonderful ingredient, and it also seems to stay fresh in my fridge for longer than most other veggies – very important when you're us. Make this and share the celery love with a friend.

Sumptuous Celery Soup

Serves 2 large bowls

Ingredients:

- 2 tbsp. olive oil (L)
- 2 cups celery fresh, chopped (L)
- 1½ cup white potatoes, chopped (L)
- 1 medium zucchini, chopped (L)
- 1 tsp. mixed dried herbs (coriander and basil) (L)
- 2 cups vegetable stock (L)
- ½ cup coconut milk (L)
- Salt, to taste (L)
- OPTIONAL: 1 tsp. sesame seeds (M)
- Mint leaves optional (L)
- 1 garlic clove, minced (L)

Instructions:

1. Sauté the onions, garlic and vegetables and dried herbs in a large saucepan for about 15 minutes; stirring frequently and adding water as needed.
2. Add the vegetable stock and bring to a boil. Pour in the coconut milk and stir well. Turn down the heat and let it simmer for about 20 minutes.
3. Transfer contents to a blender and process until very smooth.
4. Serve while warm into a bowl and garnish with mint leaves an optional sesame seeds.

Carrot and Sage Soup

Veggie goodness. A little butter on top might just finish this one off perfectly. On the SIGHI scale butter is listed as a '1' – a potentially medium histamine food that I believe most people tolerate well. I've never had any issues and actually eat quite a lot of good quality, organic butter, however in the interests of respecting the super-low-histamine nature of my cookbook I haven't included it much. So see how you go and if you are not a butter-doubter then feel free to add when appropriate.

Sage is quite a pungent herb, so lessen the quantity if you prefer a less 'herby' taste.

Serves 2 large bowls

Ingredients:

- 8-10 medium size carrots, diced (L)
- 2 parsnips, peeled and chopped (L)
- 1 stalk of celery, chopped (L)
- 1 small butternut squash, chopped (L)
- 1 tsp. dried sage (L)
- 1 tsp. turmeric (L)
- 2½ cups vegetable stock (L)
- 1 tsp. Extra Virgin Olive Oil (L) (nb, always use good quality EVOO, ghee, or butter rather than vegetable oils which may cause inflammation.)
- Salt, to taste (L)
- 3 cups water (L)

Carrot and Sage Soup

Instructions:

1. Fry the vegetables in the olive oil in a large saucepan for a few minutes and then add the turmeric and sage. Let them cook for a further 6-10 minutes.
2. Add the vegetable stock into the pan and bring to a boil. Turn down the heat and let it simmer for 25 minutes.
3. Transfer contents of the pan into a blender, add salt to taste and process until smooth.
4. Serve warm into a bowl with a knob of butter on top if you like, and with a side of cauliflower bread.

Cabbage and Zucchini Soup

You say zucchini, I say courgette, let's call the whole thing delicious. It's just a versatile veggie. And this is a sumptuous soup.

Serves 2 large bowls

Ingredients:

- 1 tbsp. olive oil (L)
- 4 medium zucchini, diced or large chunks (L)
- ½ cup cabbage, diced (L)
- ½ white onion, diced (L)
- 1 tsp. turmeric dried (L)
- 2 tsp. fresh ginger, grated (L)
- 1 clove garlic, finely chopped (L)
- ½ cup coconut milk (L)
- 2½ cups vegetable stock (L)
- Salt, to taste (L)
- Fresh parsley, for garnish (L)
- OPTIONAL: Sesame seeds, for garnish (M)

Instructions:

1. Sauté onions and spices over low heat for 4-5 minutes.
2. Add the vegetables and cook for another 5 or so minutes; stirring occasionally.
3. Add the vegetable stock and bring to a boil. Turn down the heat and let it simmer for 20-25 minutes.

Cabbage and Zucchini Soup

4. Stir in the coconut milk and cook for a few more minutes.
5. Transfer contents of the pan into a blender, add salt to taste, and process until smooth.
6. Serve warm into a bowl and add the garnishes, if using.

Creamy Broccoli Soup

Broccoli soup is so good I have two recipes for it. Delicious and nutritious. A quick note: I've tried making this soup and soups like it with stinging nettles before. Some people say that cooked stinging nettles can have a histamine-lowering effect. However I didn't find this. Perhaps it was my stinging nettle picking technique. I've listed stinging nettles as high on the food list, but if you've had success cooking stinging nettles or using them in supplement form, do let me know at www.histamineintolerance.net as I always want to consider histamine-lowering foods. Okay, back to the broccoli appreciation society.

Serves 2 large bowls

Ingredients:

- 1 medium potato, peeled and cubed (L)
- 3 cups fresh broccoli, chopped (L)
- ½ white onion, minced (L)
- 3 stalks of celery, chopped (L)
- 3 cups of vegetable broth (L)
- 1 cup unsweetened coconut milk (L)
- Salt, to taste (L)

Instructions:

1. Boil the potato until soft.
2. Meanwhile, sauté onions for a couple of minutes and then add your stock along with the veggies and bring to a boil.
3. Turn down the heat and let it simmer for 15 minutes.

Creamy Broccoli Soup

4. Transfer the contents of the pan into a blender and process until smooth.
5. Serve warm into a bowl.

Soffritto Broccoli Soup

This recipe uses soffritto, a fragrant mix of onion, carrot and celery that you can buy in frozen small chunks from the supermarket. It is the base for most soups, stews and a whole load of deliciousness in Italian cooking, and works well for most people's histamine levels. Serves 2 bowls.

Ingredients:

- 2 cups fresh broccoli, trimmed and firmly packed (L)
- 2 cups soffritto, peeled and diced (L)
- 2 cloves garlic, minced (L)
- 2 cups vegetable stock (L)
- 1 cup unsweetened non-dairy milk – see what works best in this recipe, I use coconut or oat but I know coconut has a distinct flavour (L)
- Salt and pepper to taste (L)

Instructions:

1. Steam the potato until it becomes soft.
2. Sauté garlic and onion over until they brown lightly.
3. Add the soffritto and stock and bring to a boil then let it simmer for about 15 minutes.
4. Transfer contents to blender and add the non-dairy milk. Blend until chunky (it won't take long). Serve immediately.

MAIN DISH RECIPES

INSTANT POT BEEF SHIN

The Instant Pot is a fantastic bit of kit for anyone with histamine intolerance. It's available everywhere and is quite affordable. You get the effect of slow-cooked meat, but cooked in a healthy quick pressure cooker to minimize the risk of histamine accumulation. I use the Instant Pot for lots of cooking now, and it's very versatile.

Instant Pot Beef Shin

I've only put one Instant Pot recipe in this book as I realize not everyone has one, but this is a real beauty. If you don't have an Instant Pot, you could follow this same recipe with a casserole dish although it won't cook as quickly.

Remember to always buy organic meat, especially with beef. Serve with a pea shoot salad or other veggies.

Serves 2

Ingredients:

- 500g organic beef shin (L)
- Salt, to taste (L)
- 1 tsp. turmeric (L)
- 1 tsp. sweet paprika (L)
- 1 tsp. dried oregano (L)
- 2 tsp. olive oil (L)
- 1 small cup water (L)
- OPTIONAL: 1 teaspoon Apple Cider Vinegar (M)

Instructions:

1. Put the meat in the Instant Pot inner dish, then everything else on top apart from the Apple Cider Vinegar.
2. Put the Instant Pot on 'meat' mode for 1 hour.
3. Release lid, check meat is easily shreddable (but don't shred yet).
4. Drain any excess liquid and keep this as you may want to pour over your meat as you eat. Otherwise - top tip - freeze it as it'll be a fantastic stock for something else in future.
5. Add the Apple Cider Vinegar, and then shred with a fork.
6. Eat and enjoy.

Tasty Chicken Wings

This is such a delicious way to eat meat. Remember what I said about buying organic – well it's especially important with meat. And if you don't cook your meat on the day you buy it, then you might want to freeze it and then thoroughly defrost before cooking to ensure lower histamine levels.

Serves 2 (about 5 wings each)

Ingredients:

- 2 lbs. chicken wings (L)
- Salt, to taste (L)
- OPTIONAL: 1 tsp. nutmeg (M)
- 1 tsp. sweet paprika (L)
- 1 onion, sliced (L)
- ½ leek, sliced finely (M but usually well tolerated)
- 2 cloves garlic, minced (L)
- 1 cup water (L)

Instructions:

1. Preheat the oven to 180°C.
2. Make a spice rub by combining nutmeg, salt, and garlic in a small bowl and rub it onto the chicken pieces.
3. Transfer the chicken into a roasting pan and season some more with paprika.
4. Add onions and leek and transfer the pan into the oven and cook for 40 minutes.
5. Add a cup of water into the roasting pan and let return to oven for another 40 minutes.
6. Remove from oven and let it sit briefly. You can use the juices in the pan as sauce.

"Yum Chicken" with Cottage Cheese and Rosemary

This is a filling meal that will serve 4 hungry low-histamine eaters; you may want to prepare a fresh salad to go with it. You can also use chicken breasts, but reduce the cooking time a little so it doesn't become too dry.

Note on ingredients: MCT Oil is a great ingredient and one of the cleanest sources of energy for your brain and body. I use 100% coconut MCT oil which is of course low in histamine, but you can always use olive oil instead. And FYI, sweet peppers are low in histamine but hot peppers are high. So sweet peppers it is.

Note on chicken. I love cooking chicken at home. If you go to a pub for a Sunday Roast – often the meat will sit there all day rather than be freshly cooked. I've learnt to my cost that pub/restaurant roasts are often high histamine – this really is sad as roasts are my favourite. It's always worth asking when exactly the meat was cooked when you eat out. But for now, you're cooking at home and cooking fresh, so we're all good.

Serves 4 (2 pieces of chicken each)

Ingredients:

- 8 organic chicken drumsticks or thighs (L)

- 4 large sweet potatoes (L)
- 4 tbsp. cottage cheese (L)
- A sprig or two of rosemary, chopped (L)
- ½ sweet pepper, diced (L)
- ½ zucchini, diced (L)
- 2 tsp. garlic (L)
- 1 tsp. ginger (L)
- Sea salt to taste (L)
- 3 tsp. MCT oil (L)

Instructions:

1. Combine garlic, ginger, salt, and 3 tsp. of MCT oil in a small bowl and use it the mixture to coat the chicken.
2. Preheat oven to 200°C (400°F) and prepare a baking sheet.
3. Poke each sweet potato half a dozen times and bake along with the chicken in the oven for 45 minutes. (This is easier to do with a posh double oven – so that chicken and the potatoes bake in separate ovens).
4. When you are about 15 minutes into baking the potatoes, add the sweet peppers along with the zucchini to the baking sheet.
5. Meanwhile, combine the cottage cheese and chopped rosemary in a bowl and stir well.
6. Slice each potato in two, and put some of the filling onto each one - reserve some more for garnish, you want plenty of filling.
7. Remove the vegetables from the oven and season as you wish. Serve immediately.

Oven Baked Chicken and Zucchini Toast with Herbs and Cheese

An unusual and delicious recipe. Many say ginger has histamine-reducing properties, and who am I to argue. As always, start off by going easy with the soft cheese to see if it suits you. I like to eat quite low-carb so often I'll skip the toast in this dish and simply serve it with a simple plate of fresh veggies.

Serves 2 (about ½ chicken breast each)

Ingredients:

- 1 lb. fresh chicken breast, cut into 1-inch strips (L)
- 1 tsp. freshly minced garlic (L)
- 1 tsp. freshly minced ginger (L)
- 1 tsp. extra virgin olive oil (L)
- 4 slices gluten-free toast or rice cakes (L)
- A handful of basil leaves (L)
- 4 medium zucchini, sliced (L)
- Small handful mint leaves (L)
- 3 tbsp. soft cheese (L)
- Sea salt to taste (L)

Instructions:

1. Coat the chicken strips with garlic, ginger, olive oil, and some salt. Set aside.

2. Preheat oven to 200°C (400°F) and prepare a baking sheet.
3. Arrange the zucchini slices and chicken pieces on the baking sheet and drizzle olive oil. Bake for 20 to 25 minutes (until no longer pink inside).
4. Meanwhile toast the bread. When the zucchini is ready, mash slightly with a fork, and then add cheese, olive oil, and the herbs and toss to coat well.
5. Top each toast slice with the zucchini and chicken. Garnish with herbs. Serve immediately.

Organic Beef with Herb-Based Topping

For the sake of your histamine levels, the beef you cook must be extremely fresh and a tender cut – e.g. tenderloin. A few seem to react to beef, so please buy good quality meat, and test with small quantities first. If all works out okay, you'll love this recipe. And if you react, follow some of the other dishes in this cookbook and try again in a month's time once you have lowered your histamine bucket.

For something different and because my experience is that it suits most of us, I've used black rice with this dish. It takes a while to cook, so allow about 40 minutes to cook for a unique, nutty taste along with your beef.

Cooking times can vary with beef because the thickness will vary. So I recommend a meat thermometer, which is extremely cheap.

Serves 3/4

Ingredients:

- 1 lb. fresh beef fillet, tender cut (L)
- ¼ cup cauliflower breadcrumbs (see recipe) or more, if needed (L)
- 1 tsp. fresh thyme (L)
- 1 tbsp. extra virgin olive oil (L)
- Sea salt, to taste (L)
- 1 cup black rice, cooked (L)

- A handful of pea-shoots (L)
- 1 tsp. fresh parsley (L)

Instructions:

1. Preheat oven to 200°C (400°F) and prepare a baking sheet.
2. Season the beef as you wish and transfer to the baking sheet and let it cook for about 25 minutes.
3. Meanwhile, combine the breadcrumbs, thyme, olive oil, and a little salt in a small bowl. Stir to form a pasty mixture.
4. Spread the mixture over the briefly cooked beef to coat well. Return to oven and cook until the meat thermometer reaches your desired setting. I take my inspiration from the Certified Angus Beef site, around 57°C for medium rare and 63°C for medium. The USDA recommends beef is cooked to at least medium.
5. Slice and serve with your side of cooked black rice and a pea-shoot garnish.

Honey, Rosemary, and Butter Roast Chicken with Pea Shoot Salad

I love eating small, conscious organic portions of meat, and especially chicken. Chicken is a reliable staple in terms of histamine – often better than beef which should not be aged. In the interests of looking after our environment and our histamine-levels, I always buy fresh, pasture-raised organic meat – or happy meat – and serve with a generous side salad as per the recipe. If you can't afford organic (and it is ridiculously expensive), then go for the most expensive option you can.

Serves 4 (generous servings) but can be stretched to serve 6 comfortably

Ingredients:

- 1 whole chicken (4-5 lb.) (L)
- ¾ cup honey (L)
- ¼ cup butter (L)
- 1 sprig of rosemary (L)
- 2 tbsp. cloves, minced (L)
- Side: Pea Shoot Salad (L)
- Salt, taste (L)

Instructions:

1. Preheat oven to 190°C and prepare a baking sheet.
2. Meanwhile, melt butter over medium heat in a pan and stir in the rosemary, cloves, honey, and salt. Let it cook for a couple of minutes.
3. Coat the whole chicken with the mixture and transfer to the baking sheet.
4. Roast for 60 to 75 minutes, until it is cooked through.
5. Remove from oven and let it rest for 10 minutes and then serve with a side of a large histamine-lowering pea shoot salad with a drizzle of olive oil.

Oven-Baked Whole Chicken with Mint, Basil, Zucchini and Black Rice

This is a delicious one, which can be nicely enhanced with a little apple cider vinegar. This can be a confusing ingredient. The SIGHI list (Swiss Interest Group Histamine Intolerance) categorizes apple cider vinegar as a 1 on a scale of zero to 3, but many other sites suggest it is fairly well tolerated. Test first.

Perhaps now is a good time to mention that there are studies to show black rice is a) anti-inflammatory and b) can prevent the release of histamine from mast cells.

Serves 4 (generous servings) but can be stretched to 6 comfortably.

Ingredients:

- 1 fresh roast chicken (L) (please make sure to buy very fresh) or if you'd rather 8 chicken thighs
- 1 tsp. freshly minced garlic (L)
- 1 tsp. fresh rosemary, chopped (L)
- 1 cup black rice (L)
- 2 large zucchini, diced (L)
- 1 clove garlic, finely chopped (L)
- ¼ cup single cream (L)

- ➢ 1 tbsp. fresh basil, chopped or torn (L)
- ➢ 1 tbsp. extra virgin olive oil (L)
- ➢ ½ medium white onion, diced (L)
- ➢ 1 tbsp. fresh mint, chopped (L)
- ➢ 1 tbsp. Cottage cheese (L)
- ➢ OPTIONAL: 1 tsp. apple cider vinegar (M) (go easy with the vinegar until you know whether this suits you.)
- ➢ Sea salt, to taste (L)

Instructions:

1. Preheat oven to 190°C (350°F) and prepare a baking sheet.
2. Place the chicken in a large bowl and coat well with olive oil, rosemary, garlic, and salt.
3. Transfer chicken into oven and bake for 40 minutes.
4. Meanwhile, cook the black rice as instructed.
5. In a separate pan, sauté onions and garlic for a couple of minutes and then add the zucchini. Cook for 5 minutes on medium-low heat.
6. Into the pan, add apple cider vinegar (see note above) and keep stirring for a couple more minutes.
7. Add the cream and herbs and continue stirring. When done, pour the vegetable mixture onto the cooked rice and stir lightly to mix.
8. Garnish with basil leaves and serve with the roasted chicken immediately.

Seared and Baked Lamb with Vegetables

A delicious meat dish. This is absolutely banging with a side of histamine-lowering pea shoot salad.

Serves 4 plates

Ingredients:

- 1½ lb. organic lamb fillets, fresh and lean, 1- to 2-inches thick (L)
- 1½ cups potatoes, bite-size pieces (L)
- 1 large carrot, chopped (L)
- 2 small zucchini, chopped (L)
- ½ sweet pepper, chopped (L)
- 2 tsp. MCT oil (L)

Pesto:
- ½ cup pumpkin seeds (L)
- ½ cup basil leaves (L)
- OPTIONAL: 1 tbsp. apple cider vinegar (M)
- 3 tbsp. extra virgin olive oil (L)
- ½ tsp. MCT oil (L)
- ¼ tsp. salt (L)
- OPTIONAL: 1 clove garlic, minced (L)

Instructions:

1. Preheat oven to 190°C.
2. Meanwhile, combine all pesto ingredients in a blender until smooth. Set aside.

3. In a hot skillet with a touch of MCT oil, sear the lamb for a couple of minutes on each side.
4. In the same skillet, add a little more oil and add all the vegetables.
5. Cover with foil and transfer to oven to bake for 25-30 minutes.
6. Remove from oven and top with pesto to form a crust. Return into the oven to bake for another 20 minutes until lamb is cooked well.
7. Serve immediately with a side of a histamine-lowering pea shoot salad, a drizzle of MCT oil and some sea salt.

Sweet Paprika Crusted Cod

I deliberated long and hard over whether to include a fish dish in this cookbook. Fish and histamine can be problematic, unless it is extremely fresh or frozen straight after being caught. So try and ensure it is as fresh as possible, and test with small quantities first. I am lucky to buy fish from an awesome company called Seafresh in the UK that freezes fish at sea - if you live in the UK try them out. If you live elsewhere, let me know if you find a good 'frozen-at-sea' supplier so I can recommend them.

If fish does agree with you, you'll love this really simple take on a 'fish dinner' which will go down well with all the family. I'm using frozen fish here for freshness and add a lovely gluten-free crumb topping flavoured with sweet paprika. If you prefer not to use butter, then swap out for extra virgin olive oil. Serve with chunky chips or sweet potato chips and your favourite vegetables.

Serves 2

Ingredients:

- 2 frozen-at-sea cod fillets (L)
- ¼ slice of gluten-free bread (fresh or frozen) blended to breadcrumbs (L)
- ¼ tsp. garlic powder (L)
- 1 tsp. butter (M)
- 1 tsp. sweet paprika (L)
- Salt, to taste (L)

Instructions:

1. Defrost the fish thoroughly. Preheat the oven to 200C. Once at temperature place your cod fillets into an ovenproof dish and cover with foil. Bake for 15 minutes.
2. Combine the gluten-free breadcrumbs, sweet paprika, garlic powder, butter and salt in a bowl and mix well.
3. Remove the fish from the oven and pat on the breadcrumb mixture to form a crust. Return to the oven and bake for a further 15 minutes, or until the fish is thoroughly cooked through.
4. Plate up with your chips and vegetables, and serve immediately.

Vegan Power Dinner

I like meat and do believe that consciously sourced it can play a role in a healthy diet. But I also like to eat meat-free, vegetarian and vegan meals, and that can provide a challenge on the low-histamine diet as so many nuts, cheeses and cheese substitutes are out. So I present to you my Vegan Power Dinner.

Serves 2 bowls

Ingredients:

- ½ cup quinoa, uncooked (L)
- ¼ zucchini, sliced (L)
- ½ cup potatoes cut into halves (L)
- ½ cup sweet pepper, sliced (L)
- 2 radishes, sliced (L)
- ½ cup lettuce, shredded (L)
- ½ cup carrot, grated (L)
- 1 tbsp. extra virgin olive oil (L)
- 1 tsp. dried basil (L)
- Salt, to taste (L)

DRESSING:
- 3 tbsp. olive oil (L)
- 1 tsp. raw honey (L)
- OPTIONAL: 1 tsp. apple cider vinegar (M)

TOPPINGS:
- 1 tsp. pumpkin seeds (L)
- 1 tsp. parsley, chopped (L)
- 1 tsp. shallots sliced (L)

Instructions:

1. Preheat oven to 200°C (400°F) and prepare a baking sheet.
2. Arrange the vegetables (except lettuce and carrots) in the baking sheet and drizzle olive oil and sprinkle seasoning. Transfer to oven and bake for half an hour.
3. Meanwhile cook quinoa as instructed on the package. Transfer into a serving bowl. Set aside.
4. Combine dressing ingredients and stir well. Set aside.
5. Plate your serving bowl by adding your grated carrots and lettuce to the quinoa.
6. Add the baked veggies and drizzle the dressing. Top with desired toppings. Serve immediately.

Maple Baked Ricotta and Butternut Squash

When I started low histamine, I was disappointed at having to restrict cheese. I don't want to eat cheese all the time but it's a nice treat. Since then I've closely looked at my low histamine food list and I seem to tolerate soft cheeses well. They are low on the SIGHI scale too, so see how you go with this delicious ricotta recipe.

Serves 2

Ingredients:

Herb oil:
- 2 tbsp. olive oil (L)
- 1 tbsp. fresh thyme (L)
- Salt, to taste (L)

Vegetables:
- 1 package ricotta (about 250g) (L)
- 1 small butternut squash, large slices (L)
- 1 small dumpling squash, large pieces (L)
- 5 sprigs broccoli (L)
- 2 tbsp. fresh thyme (L)
- 3 rosemary sprigs (L)
- 1 sweet pepper, large pieces (L)
- 1 tbsp. maple syrup (L)
- 1 tbsp. olive oil (L)
- Salt, to taste (L)

Instructions:

1. Preheat oven to 190°C and prepare a baking sheet.
2. Transfer all herb oil ingredients into a pestle and mortar and mash well together. Transfer into a small bowl and set aside.
3. Spread out all the vegetables evenly on the baking sheet and add the ricotta and rosemary in between the vegetables. Drizzle 1 tbsp. of olive oil over the traybake, and the maple syrup over the ricotta.
4. Season to your liking and then bake for about 40 minutes.
5. Once the vegetable mixture has baked well, drizzle the herb oil and serve immediately.

Zucchini, Basil, and Mint Rice Pasta

This is a lovely recipe on its own. And with the mozzarella, it gets even better. See how you fare with the mozzarella. Most of the food lists hard cheese as very high histamine (with the blue ones the worst), but list soft cheeses as lower histamine. I recently ran a Mozzarella poll on www.histamineintolerance.net and 75% of people were positive about Mozzarella on a low-histamine diet.

Serves 2 plates

Ingredients:

- 2 cups rice pasta, cooked (L)
- 2 large zucchini (1 sliced and 1 grated) (L)
- 1 tbsp. olive oil (L)
- OPTIONAL: ½ white onion, chopped (M)
- 1 tsp. cloves (L)
- ¼ cup single cream (L)
- 2 tbsp. fresh mint, chopped (L)
- 2 tbsp. fresh basil, chopped (L)
- OPTIONAL: 1 tsp. apple cider vinegar (M)
- Salt, to taste (L)
- OPTIONAL: Mozzarella (M)

Instructions:

1. Sauté onions for a couple of minutes and then add the sliced zucchini. Cook on a low-medium heat for a few minutes until it softens and then add the grated zucchini.

2. Add the vinegar and stir well.
3. Separately cook the pasta (I love rice pasta and also pea pasta as an alternative).
4. Add cream and herbs to the pasta and stir through. Then add the cooked zucchini.
5. Serve immediately with the mozzarella, if using, and garnish with basil leaves. Enjoy!

Butternut Squash Gnocchi

I was lucky enough to holiday in the Caribbean (I am not gloating, honest!). And in Barbados, they cook with Cassava all the time. Cassava pops up time and again in this cookbook, and that's because it's a versatile, low-GI, low-histamine alternative to more conventional, stodgier flour. Thankfully, you can buy cassava flour easily in any good health shop or online. Get ready for a Caribbean inspired low-histamine taste sensation when it combines with the butternut squash.

Serves 4 plates

Ingredients:

- 5 cups butternut squash, skinned and cut into chunks (steamed) (L)
- 2 cups cassava flour. (Use brown rice flour or coconut if you can't source cassava) (L)
- 1 tsp. olive oil (L)
- Himalayan salt to taste

Instructions:

1. Into a large bowl, add the steamed butternut squash and flour.
2. Stir well to form a doughy mixture. Roll some gnocchi-shaped pieces with your hands and set aside.

3. Boil some water, then drop in your gnocchi pieces and let them cook until they float to the surface. It doesn't take long - between 4 and 6 minutes.
4. Drain the gnocchi then drizzle with a tiny bit of olive oil, sprinkle some good-quality salt on and you are good to go.

Coconut Quinoa Risotto

Who needs sharing plates when you can eat it all yourself?

Serves a cosy plate for 1.

Ingredients:

- 1 cup quinoa, cooked (L)
- ½ large zucchini, chopped (L)
- 1 cup coconut milk (L)
- 1½ tsp. turmeric (L)
- 1 tsp. dried thyme (L)
- 1 tbsp. extra virgin olive oil (L)
- 1 medium or large carrot, chopped (L)
- 1 sweet pepper, chopped (L)
- Salt, to taste (L)
- Parsley, for garnish (L)
- OPTIONAL: 1 tsp. apple cider vinegar (M)

Instructions:

1. Fry the vegetables in olive oil for 5 minutes and then add the herbs.
2. Add quinoa and coconut milk into the frying pan, bring to a boil and then reduce the heat.
3. Add apple cider vinegar and stir through. Let it cook over low heat for about 10-15 minutes.
4. Season then serve and garnish immediately.

Cheesy Baked Butternut Squash Risotto

A flavourful main dish or side-dish that lets the oven do the work! Vegetables and herbs are combined with arborio rice, and a good stir of cream cheese for a healthy comfort food dinner. If you prefer not to use cream cheese, it will still be good! Butternut squash can be quite the task to chop, so look out for frozen chopped butternut squash which is admittedly lazy but saves lots of time as well as maintains freshness.

Serve 2 as a main dish or 4 as a side dish

Ingredients:

- 2 tsps. extra virgin olive oil (L)
- ½ white onion (L)
- ½ garlic clove (L)
- 150g arborio rice (L)
- 2 cups butternut squash (L)
- 1 cup broccoli (L)
- 1 tsp. dried thyme (L)
- 2 tbsps. cream cheese (M)
- 2½ cups vegetable stock (L)
- pinch, salt (L)

Instructions:

1. Preheat the oven to 200°C.
2. In an ovenproof pan, add the olive oil and fry the onion and garlic for 4-5 minutes on a low heat until

Cheesy Baked Butternut Squash Risotto

softened. Add the butternut squash and broccoli, dried thyme and salt, and cook for a further 4-5 minutes.
3. Pour in the rice and stir well so combined. Then pour in the vegetable stock, and stir well again.
4. Transfer your dish to the oven and bake the risotto for 30 minutes, removing from the oven halfway through to stir well. Add a little more stock or water if need be.
5. Remove from the oven and stir through the cream cheese.
6. Serve immediately and enjoy!

Honey Roasted Pumpkin Quinoa

Honey Roasted Pumpkin Quinoa

Serves 1 bowl

Ingredients:

- 1 cup pumpkin, diced (L)
- 2 tsp. extra virgin olive oil (L)
- Honey, to taste (L)
- OPTIONAL: ½ tsp. cinnamon (M)
- ½ tsp. dried basil (L)
- ½ tsp. dried coriander (L)
- ½ tsp. turmeric powder (L)
- ½ roasted sweet pepper, diced (L)
- ½ roasted zucchini, sliced (L)
- 1 tsp. extra virgin olive oil (L)
- ½ cup quinoa, cooked (L)
- 1 tsp. dried mixed herbs (coriander and basil) (L)
- 1 tbsp. pumpkin seeds (L)
- OPTIONAL: 1 tsp. sesame seeds (M)
- 2 cups rocket (L)
- 1 tbsp. mint leaves, chopped (L)
- 1 tbsp. pomegranate seeds (L)
- Salt, to taste (L)

Instructions:

1. Preheat oven to 190°C and prepare a baking sheet.
2. Spread out the pumpkin onto the baking sheet and coat with honey, olive oil, spices, and herbs. Add the sweet pepper and zucchini to the baking sheet and drizzle with a little olive oil. Bake for half an hour.
3. Start warming the quinoa, and enjoy a bit of downtime.
4. Stir the mixed herbs into the warm cooked quinoa and set aside.
5. Begin plating the quinoa, roasted vegetables, and rocket. Top with the pomegranate seeds, and pumpkin and sesame seeds and season to your liking. Serve immediately.

Cherry, Blackberry, Cottage Cheese Salad

Yes, quite a daring combination. Sometimes with low histamine recipes you gotta get inventive. Let me know what you think, I love this, but if it's too way out for you there are simpler salads.

Serves 1 large bowl

Ingredients:

- 1 cup cottage cheese (L)
- 2 cups lettuce, firmly packed (L)
- 2 tbsp. cherries, de-stoned (L)
- 2 tbsp. blackberries (L)
- 1 tbsp. basil leaves, chopped (L)
- 1 tbsp. pumpkin seeds (L)

DRESSING:
- 2 tbsp. extra virgin olive oil (L)
- OPTIONAL: 1 tsp. apple cider vinegar (M)
- OPTIONAL: 1 tsp. honey (L)
- Salt, to taste (L)

Instructions:

1. In a small bowl, combine all the dressing ingredients and mix well. Set aside.
2. Arrange the lettuce and basil on a plate and then top with cottage cheese, and the cherries and blackberries.

Cherry, Blackberry, Cottage Cheese Salad

3. Season to your liking and then drizzle the dressing over the salad. The honey in the dressing is optional, though I find this adventurous salad quite sweet enough without. Serve immediately.

Rice, Pea Shoot and Pomegranate Salad

Cooled white rice is a brilliant inflammation hack. It works like this. You cook it with 3 tbsp. coconut oil, then drain and cool in the fridge. The American Chemical Society says rice cooked this way produces a smaller spike in blood sugar because resistant starch is created when it cools. This means you won't get the carb crashes you might get from normal rice. It also tastes great. Thanks to my friends at Bulletproof for the inspiration for the rice part of this dish.

The rice and Pea Shoots are some of my favourite ingredients. Pea Shoots are a) delicious in a salad, and b) supposedly one of the finest histamine-lowering foods. I buy them by the bucket-load and are taking a tentative step towards growing them as well. If you can grow your own, even better. In this recipe, they're more of a garnish, but pea shoots are a staple in our fridge, and get wheeled out in a number of the dishes you'll see in this recipe book.

Serves 1 bowl

Ingredients:

- ½ cup rice, cooked with coconut oil and cooled (L)
- 2 tbsp. white onion, diced (L)
- 1 tbsp. pumpkin seeds (L)
- 2 tbsp. fresh mint leaves, chopped (L)
- ½ sweet pepper, diced (L)
- ½ small cucumber, diced (L)

Rice, Pea Shoot and Pomegranate Salad

- 2 tbsp. pomegranate seeds (L)
- 2 tbsp. fresh parsley, chopped (L)
- 2 tbsp. pea shoots (L)

DRESSING:
- 1 tbsp. extra virgin olive oil (L)
- OPTIONAL: 1 tsp. apple cider vinegar (M)
- Maple syrup, to taste (L)
- Salt, to taste (L)

Instructions:

1. In a bowl, combine all dressing ingredients and mix well. Set aside.
2. Combine all the other ingredients in a bowl and toss to mix well.
3. Drizzle the dressing over the salad. Serve immediately.

SECRET SAUCES

Low-Histamine Ketchup

Introducing my 'Secret Sauce' section. In the first book, Histamine Intolerance Explained, one of my features running through the book was a 'Secret Sauce' section where I gave you some secret histamine tips you wouldn't find anywhere else. Now I've decided to actually come up with some secret sauces. Sauces can be a challenge on the histamine diet, because so many contain vinegar. If out and about I might allow myself a little mustard, but sometimes I'll feel it the next day. So here are a few Secret Sauces you can have any time.

And I'm going to boldly state something here. This homemade low-histamine ketchup is better than the real thing! I mean, there's less sugar, but it's just so delicious. And it's all without tomatoes which are unfortunately very problematic in terms of histamine. The not-so-secret ingredients are a) carrots (a widely-used tomato substitute - even our local pizza takeaway now offers pizzas with carrot rather than tomato), and b) ginger, which gives this a sensational little kick. I list ginger as low histamine in the list, and while the respected SIGHI scale lists this as a '1' rather than a '0', it notes that small amounts are well tolerated.

I tend to make a batch of this and then freeze anything that isn't used. One final thought - why not try this ketchup with the Burger Bites? They go great together.

Serves 2 cups of ketchup

Ingredients:

- 2 onions (L)
- 1 tsp. extra virgin olive oil (L)
- 4 large carrots, cut into small pieces (L)
- 1 medium-sized apple, peeled and cut into quarters (L)
- Salt, to taste (L)
- ¼ tsp. turmeric (L)
- ½ tsp. garlic powder (L)
- ½ tsp. of sweet paprika (L)
- 1 knob of ginger (L)
- 1 dried apricot (unsulphured) (L)
- ¼ cup water (L)
- Dash of stevia (L)
- 1 tbsp. Apple Cider Vinegar (M)

Instructions:

1. Chop the onions and the ginger. Make sure these are chopped finely. You could use a blender.
2. Sauté onions in the olive oil. After a minute or two, put in the ginger until it all browns.
3. Meanwhile, steam the carrot and apple pieces until they are soft.
4. Put the carrots and apples in the blender along with the remaining ingredients. Add just a dash of stevia, too sweet and you'll have to start again!
5. Combine everything together until smooth. Add salt or more stevia if needed.
6. Enjoy. It's not quite the same colour as a bottle of Heinz Tomato Ketchup, but it's perhaps even more delish. Freeze what you don't use for next time.

No-Yogurt Honey Mint Dip

This one is a bit naughty, but it's a gorgeous secret sauce for a pudding with some fruit. Coconut cream takes the place of yogurt to make it low histamine.

Serves 1 cup of dip

Ingredients:

- 5 tbsp. organic coconut cream (L)
- 1 tbsp. good quality honey (L)
- A handful of fresh mint leaves, finely chopped (L)

Instructions:

1. You don't need the blender for this one. Just get a bowl, combine all the ingredients and stir thoroughly.
2. Serve immediately with a side of fresh low-histamine fruit (consult the food list in this book for details).

Pomegranate, Garlic and Ginger Salad Sauce

Pomegranate is an excellent low-histamine ingredient. So I thought, how can I work this into a delicious recipe I can use again and again. Enter my Pomegranate Garlic and Ginger Salad Sauce. Not strictly a dressing, nor a sauce, but what the hell, I've put it in my Secret Sauces section anyway.

It's especially easy as you can buy pomegranate juice in any health store and don't have to go to the faff of deseeding, squeezing, juicing and so on.

Serves ¾ to 1 cup of dressing

Ingredients:

- 1 cup of pomegranate juice (L)
- 1 tbsp. extra virgin olive oil (L)
- ¼ tsp. freshly minced garlic (L)
- ¼ tsp. freshly minced ginger (L)
- A pinch of salt (L)

Instructions:

1. Combine the ingredients in a blender. Make sure the garlic and the ginger are cut finely.
2. Give a very quick whizz. It won't take long.
3. Enjoy. Sauce or dressing, you decide.

Sweet Paprika Spiced Tahini Dressing

Tahini is a versatile ingredient made from sesame seeds. It makes a tasty dressing for salads or hot dishes. It is listed as medium on my food list and I confess I only have it occasionally. This is one I've changed my mind on a little since the first version of this book in 2020. But many are okay with tahini, so I've left the recipe in. Please test this out in very small quantities at first. You can always have it as it is, which is delicious, but adding sweet paprika gives a nice hum of extra flavour. Adjust the amount of sweet paprika to your taste.

Serves ¼ cup

Ingredients:

- ¼ cup tahini (M)
- 2 tbsp. warm water (L)
- 1 tbsp. sweet paprika (L)
- pinch salt (L)

Instructions:

1. Add all the ingredients to a bowl and stir well. The tahini will initially look gritty, but keep stirring and it will become a creamy dressing.
2. Sprinkle a little more sweet paprika on top to make it look fancy. Impress your guests with how delicious the low-histamine diet is.

DRINKS RECIPES

Fiery Carrot and Turmeric Juice

Now onto some delicious low-histamine juices you can enjoy any time. This fiery juice requires a juicer, but is well worth the inevitable clean-up afterwards. Just don't spill it on your best white tablecloth. Contains histamine-lowering pea shoots abundant in DAO, as well as apples and ginger.

Time to drink your medicine!

Serves 1 glass

Ingredients:

- A handful of pea shoots (L)
- 1 small knob of fresh peeled turmeric (L)
- 3 big carrots (L)
- 2 chopped-up apples (L)
- 1 tbsp. of freshly sliced ginger (L)

Instructions:

1. Clean and prepare the ingredients.
2. Push each through a juicer.
3. Serve in a tall glass and enjoy.

Celery and Ginger Juice

So many good ingredients. Juicing is a bit of a faff at times, but the end result is so worth it. Unfortunately our local juice bars like to make their drinks very sweet – whereas for the real health benefits, I like to have mostly veggies in my Celery and Ginger Juice.

Serves 1 large glass

Ingredients:

- 2 handfuls of mint leaves (L)
- 1 tsp. of fresh thyme (L)
- 1 tbsp. freshly sliced ginger (L)
- 1 cup of celery stalks, trimmed and cut (L)
- A handful of pea shoots (L)
- A handful of lamb's lettuce (L)
- 2 medium apples cut into quarters (L)
- ½ cup water or more if needed (L)
- Stevia, to taste but the ginger gives it a nice kick (optional) (L)

Instructions:

1. Clean and prepare the ingredients.
2. Push each through a juicer.
3. Stir in the stevia if needed. Serve in a tall glass and enjoy.

Ginger and Green Apple Drink

Variations on a theme here, but this really is juice as medicine, hence lots of these yummy drinks. If your histamine bucket is overflowing, make yourself this drink and slowly feel yourself start to recover. If you are not feeling good, I sympathise, as I've been there many times in this journey. Histamine lowering ingredients include apple, pea shoots and ginger root. Please do remember to check out the supplements section in Histamine Intolerance Explained for instant ways to start healing. And always consult your doctor first.

Serves 2 glasses

Ingredients:

- 2 apples (L)
- 1½ cup coconut water (L)
- 2 cups pea shoots (L)
- 2 tsp. fresh ginger, or from frozen also fine (L)

Instructions:

1. Combine all ingredients in your blender.
2. Give it a quick whizz.
3. Drink.

Sweet Melon and Cucumber Smoothie

In this recipe, I've offered you the option of Monk Fruit sweetener to taste. I don't really think it needs it, but Monk Fruit is a great ingredient, a very low sugar alternative to, well, sugar. It's very sweet and a good natural option.

Serves 1 large glass

Ingredients:

- 1 cup sweet melon (L)
- 1 cup of wonderful histamine-lowering pea shoots (L)
- 1 cucumber, sliced (L)
- Monk Fruit sweetener, to taste (L)
- ½ cup water (L)

Instructions:

1. Whack all the ingredients in your blender.
2. Give it a quick buzz.
3. Drink and enjoy.

Basil and Blackberry Potion

Fresh and light, though I provide the option of ground flaxseed to bulk it out. This might be a good recipe to add a favourite low histamine protein powder for extra nutrition post workout. Also works well with blueberries instead of blackberries.

Serves 1 large glass

Ingredients:

- 1 cup fresh blackberries (L)
- 1 cup oat milk (L)
- A handful of fresh basil leaves (L)
- OPTIONAL: 1 tbsp. ground flaxseed for extra substance (L)
- OPTIONAL: your low-histamine protein powder of choice (L)

Instructions:

1. Combine all ingredients in a high-speed blender.
2. Process until very smooth.
3. Serve immediately.

Sweet Melon, Peach, and Chia Smoothie

Chia seeds make a welcome return in this final smoothie. One more interesting fact on histamine from me. (Well, I think it's interesting). Many people with histamine intolerance report that they find it hard to hydrate, and often feel very thirsty. If this is you, go easy with the chia seeds and leave the smoothie a while after blending to to allow the chia seeds to take on the liquid. As I say, this is based mostly on my experience (plus other anecdotal), and I think it's worth passing on.

Serves 2 glasses

Ingredients:

- 1½ cups sweet melon chunks (L)
- 1 peach de-stoned (L)
- ½ cup coconut milk (L)
- OPTIONAL: 1 tsp. almond butter (M)
- 2 tsp. chia seeds, milled (L)
- Ice cubes (L)

Instructions:

1. Combine all ingredients in a high-powered blender.
2. Process until very smooth.
3. Serve immediately or leave for a little while to allow the chia seeds to thicken.

DESSERT RECIPES

Uncle Steve's Caribbean Pone

Our Uncle Steve lives in Barbados, and when we went to stay the whole house smelt sensational. It turned out he had been cooking a local dish called pone for three hours, with smells of cassava, ginger and spices wafting on the warm air through the house. Pone is a gooey, squidgy cross between a flapjack and a cake that Barbadians love, and who can blame them.

Now Uncle Steve is the master of pone, and I wouldn't even pretend that this is on his level, but it's tasty all the same. The secret is cassava, a magical ingredient I've mentioned already that will serve you well in your low-histamine life. Steve grates the cassava himself (an arduous task that seemed to take most of the day). I've not got his stamina so I have used coarse Cassava Flour, easily available online. That did the trick just fine.

Please note - raisins are low histamine in this book and on the respected SIGHI scale, however some people find them problematic, so go cautiously. Ginger and Vanilla can be problematic but tend to be well tolerated - go cautiously. In addition, most pone recipes seem to contain a lot of sugar. This recipe contains none at all. I just use a little stevia instead, and honestly, it works just as well. It's still not the lowest carb recipe in here, but it's totally delicious, and if you have a small slice at a time it'll last for ages. Of course, that is not going to happen. Uncle Steve, I hope I made you proud with this low-histamine pone, and thank you again for the inspiration.

If you would like to see a step-by-step cooking guide in pictures for this Caribbean Pone, head over to the blog on the website. And this is another dish that freezes well.

Serves 12

Ingredients:

- 3 cups (385g) coarse cassava flour (L)
- 2 cups (200g) desiccated coconut (L)
- 1 serving of powdered stevia (L)
- ¼ lb. (113g) seedless raisins (L)
- 2 eggs (M)

Uncle Steve's Caribbean Pone

- 3 cups (675ml) coconut milk (L)
- ¼ lb. (113g) butter (melted) (L)
- ½ teaspoon cinnamon (L)

OPTIONAL
- 1 teaspoon vanilla powder (not essence) (M but tends to be well tolerated)
- ½ teaspoon ginger (L and tends to be well tolerated)
- 1 teaspoon nutmeg (M)

Instructions:

1. Mix your dry ingredients together in a bowl.
2. Melt the butter, and then combine in a separate bowl with milk and beaten eggs.
3. Add the wet ingredients to the dry and mix well.
4. Pour the mixture into a well-greased dish.
5. Bake at 300°F for 1½ hours or until a knife comes out clean.
6. Remove from oven and allow to cool for 20-30 minutes. Then enjoy.

Histahappy Slice

Don't ask me why I called this recipe Histahappy Slice. Okay, do. It's because it makes me happy. It does contain coconut sugar – something I tend to keep to a minimum in my cooking, but in this instance I know it's worth it.

While on the subject of baking, Beth O' Hara has a terrific low-histamine scone recipe on her site MastCell360 which I regularly cook and urge you to check out.

Okay, back to the slice. Serves 8 to 12 pieces.

Ingredients:

- 2 cups cassava flour (L)
- ½ cup coconut sugar (L)
- 1 cup butter (L)
- ½ tsp. nutmeg (M but normally well tolerated)
- ½ tsp. ginger powder (L, though occasionally problematic)

Instructions:

1. Preheat oven to 165°C and prepare a baking sheet.
2. Melt the butter, then combine with the coconut sugar, ginger and nutmeg into a bowl and use an electric whisk to cream well.
3. Add the cassava flour into the mixture and mix.
4. Time to get your rolling pin out! Roll into a good slice depth, then cut into slices.
5. Bake for at least 25 minutes but with cassava it often depends on the batch of flour, and may well need longer.

Histahappy Slice

6. Remove the bake from the oven, and let it cool for at least 20 minutes. This is an important step, try to resist eating straight away
7. Congratulations, you've showed admirable restraint. It's time to tuck into your slice(s).

Blackberry and Cherry Crisp

A hit with all the family, especially in the colder months. This blackberry and cherry is easy to make and perfect for a weekend dessert.

Blackberry and Cherry Crisp

Serves 4

Ingredients:

- 3 cups blackberries (L)
- 1 cup cherries (L)
- 1½ cups oats (L)
- 50g butter (L)
- 2 tbsp. maple syrup (L)
- 1 serving stevia (L)
- 2 tbsp. pumpkin seeds (L)

Instructions:

1. Preheat the oven to 180C.
2. Spread the fruit in an even layer in an ovenproof dish and drizzle on the maple syrup.
3. In a large bowl add the other ingredients and then rub the butter through the oat mixture so that it combines.
4. Sprinkle evenly over the fruit and bake for 30-40 minutes so the topping is light golden brown.
5. Serve immediately and enjoy!

Blueberry "Ice Cream"

This is a delicious and very easy dish that works well with a high-speed blender. I've called it 'ice cream' but if you leave it overnight it'll be too hard, so serve immediately or leave in the freezer for just a couple of hours.

Our lives changed for ever when we invested in a decent blender, and they're surprisingly good value. We went for a Ninja blender, although others are available and you can spend a fortune on the top end ones. This recipe won't work so well with a NutriBullet.

As noted previously – I've used coconut milk in this and many recipes, but it can be interchangeable with other non-dairy milks depending on your own low-histamine preferences and what agrees with you the most. I always pay extra for organic and less ingredients.

Serves 2 dessert glasses

Ingredients:

- 1 cup frozen blueberries (L)
- 1 cup frozen coconut (L)
- 1 serving stevia (L)
- 1 cup coconut milk (L)

Instructions:

1. Combine all the ingredients in a high-powered blender and pulse until completely smooth.
2. Serve immediately or freeze in a silicon container to firm up a bit more.

Blackberry Coconut Popsicles

A fun fruity treat for summer days, these will go down well with kids and adults alike. And they are relatively healthy. Popsicle moulds are super-easy to find and you might find you start to get inventive with them.

Serves 6-7 popsicles

Ingredients:

- 2 cups blackberries (L)
- 1 400ml can of coconut milk (L)
- 1 serving of stevia (L)

Instructions:

1. Add all the ingredients to a NutriBullet or blender and pulse blend for 5-10 seconds or until the ingredients are all combined.
2. Pour into your popsicle moulds (it is easier to first pour the mixture into a jug and then into the moulds).
3. Freeze for at least 6 hours to set.
4. Enjoy!

CHIA JAM

Who says you can't have jam on a low-histamine diet? This one works fine for me, though I would add two caveats. Firstly, test this recipe in small quantities on yourself and see how you react. Second, don't leave the jam for months like a normal jam. Treat it as fresh and use it within 2/3 days to keep the histamine levels low. I recommend with the cauliflower bread from earlier.

Serves 2-3 cups

Ingredients:

- 3 cups blueberries (L)
- 2 tbsp. chia seeds (L)
- 1 tbsp. honey or 1 serving of stevia (L)

Instructions:

1. Cook the blueberries over low heat in a saucepan with ½ cup of water until just about half the berries form a thick liquid. It usually takes about 8-10 minutes.
2. Add the honey and stir well.
3. Turn off the heat and stir in the chia seeds. Let it cool and expand.
4. Store in an air-tight container and in the fridge.

List of Ingredients Used

Agave syrup
Almond butter
Apple
Apples Artichoke
Baby carrots
Baking powder
Bay leaves
Blackberries
Breadcrumbs
Brown rice
Butter
Cabbage
Carrot
Cauliflower
Celery
Cherry
Chia seeds
Chicken marrow bones
Chinese leaf cabbage
Cinnamon stick
Coconut
Coconut flakes
Coconut milk
Cod fillets
Cottage cheese

All spice
Almonds
Apple cider vinegar
Asian cabbage
Baby corn
Basil
Beet
Blueberries
Broccoli
Brown rice flour
Butternut squash
Cantaloupe melon
Carrots
Cassava flour
Celery stalks
Cherries
Chicken
Chicken wings with skin
Cinnamon
Clove
Coconut cream
Coconut flour
Coconut oil
Coriander
Courgette

List of Ingredients Used

- Cucumber
- Dates
- Egg
- Farmer's cheese
- Flaxseeds
- Frozen peaches
- Geheimrats cheese
- Goat milk
- Green apple
- Halibut
- Hemp seeds
- Ice
- Leafy greens
- Lettuce
- Maca
- Mint
- Mozzarella
- Oats
- Onion
- Parsley
- Peach
- Pear
- Pink Himalayan salt
- Pomegranate
- Potatoes
- Pumpkin seed butter
- Quinoa
- Raisins
- Red apple
- Red onion
- Date
- Dumpling squash
- Extra virgin olive oil
- Fennel bulb
- Frozen blackberries
- Garlic
- Ginger
- Goji berries
- Green cabbage
- Heavy whipping cream
- Honey
- Kale
- Leek
- Macadamia nuts
- Maple syrup
- Mixed herbs
- Nutmeg
- Olive oil
- Oregano
- Parsnip
- Peaches
- Pepper
- Pistachios
- Pomegranate seeds
- Pumpkin
- Pumpkin seeds
- Radishes
- Rapeseed oil
- Red beet
- Rice

Histamine Intolerance Cookbook

- Rice pasta
- Rocket
- Sage
- Sea salt
- Shallot
- Spirulina
- Sweet melon
- Sweet pepper
- Sweetcorn
- Thyme
- Turmeric
- Vegetable broth
- Vegetable stock
- Watercress
- Whey protein powder
- White potatoes
- Wild rice
- Ricotta
- Rosemary
- Salt
- Sesame seeds
- Shallots
- Squash
- Sweet paprika
- Sweet potato
- Tahini
- Turkey
- Unsweetened non-dairy milk
- Vegetable oil
- Water
- Whey
- White onion
- Whole grain
- Zucchini

Final Words

I hope you've truly loved the recipes in this cookbook. However I'm willing to bet that you've seen one or two recipes in here with ingredients that you might consider to be medium/high histamine. That's the problem with histamine intolerance - it's so individual. As you know, I've used what I believe to be the best information possible to come up with this Histamine Intolerance Cookbook. However, I realize that there is always room for improvement; so, if you think that that something isn't quite right I am committed to making this even better.

You can let me know through the site, and I'd LOVE an honest review or even just a simple one-tap rating. That's how I get the word out to more people about histamine intolerance.

Histamine Intolerance Cookbook

I update this cookbook as needed. It's a learning journey for me too – I are interested in getting my histamine levels down just like you. So please do contact me at The Histamine Intolerance Site (www.histamineintolerance.net) with what you like and what you'd change. I hope you feel healthy and happy eating these low-histamine creations, and I wish you the best on your healing journey.

For more content, check out the website, and my podcast Zestology, where I've interviewed lots of low-histamine experts like Beth O'Hara, Dr. Tina Peers, Dilly Kumar, and many more.

What's Next?

Come and take my 14-Day Low Histamine Challenge (www.histamineintolerance.net/challenge). You might be surprised at how much better you feel. (I was!). You'll find videos, downloads, and a supportive community to help you through it.

And if you really want to go deep, take my signature health course combining my two areas of expertise

The Healthy AF Method (www.tonywrighton.com/healthy) teaches you to deeply relax and initiate healing by activating the parasympathetic nervous system. (Without this deep state of calm we can't properly heal - and that's a massive problem with histamine intolerance.)

On this program, you'll immediately start to feel better and less anxious about your health. (I wrote it because I needed it!) Then in the 'Long-Term Transformation' section, engage in a profound shift encompassing environment, behavior, capabilities, values, beliefs, and identity. Ensure lasting change through a complete lifestyle overhaul.

Finally, you'll find a supportive community and loads of histamine-based chat, as - surprise, surprise - a lot of people with histamine intolerance find stress is their number one trigger.

Printed in Poland
by Amazon Fulfillment
Poland Sp. z o.o., Wrocław